This book belongs to:

_____

Phone:

_____

Email:

_____

Address:

_____

_____

vision | ˈviZHən|
noun
the faculty or state of being
able to see:

the ability to think about or plan
the future with imagination or wisdom

a mental image of what the future
will or could be like

A product of the
Coach in a Book Series™

*****

Creating answers and strategies
to help people get unstuck, succeed and experience breakthrough.

Author: Tarsha L. Campbell
Certified Life & Empowerment Coach

www.TarshaCampbellEmpowers.com

www.MyNextStepVisionBoardJournal.com

2022 Edition

Copyright © 2021-2022 Tarsha L. Campbell
ISBN 978-1-7367927-6-6

Book interior layout & cover design:
Tarsha L. Campbell

Published by:
DOMINIONHOUSE Publishing & Design, LLC
P.O. Box 681938 | Orlando, Florida 32868 | 407.703.4800
www.mydominionhouse.com

The Lord gave the Word: great was the company
of those who published it. (Psalm 68:11)

Table of Contents

A PERSON WITH A VISION HAS THE POWER TO CREATE THEIR WORLD

AND LEAVE

A LEGACY THAT IMPACTS

GENERATIONS TO COME.

INTRODUCTION

●●●

Why This Journal-Planner Was Created

Vision is a powerful thing! Vision gives you the power to look beyond your current situation and see into the future. Everything you see around you started with a vision. The houses we live in, the cars we drive, the technology we use—the list goes on and on. Vision is the undeniable force that allows you to step out of today, venture into tomorrow to view future possibilities, and then step back into your present to recreate what you have seen. Isn't that fascinating?

In Genesis 1:26-27, God speaks of making man (including woman, too) in His image and likeness. Without a doubt, being able to envision what could be is one of the characteristics that make us like Him. As descendants of the Divine Creator, we all have the power to envision what could be and to then take the necessary actions to make that a reality.

From the positive relationships we long for, the material things we need, and the lifestyles we want and dream about—to the finances that fund the currents of our lives, and the health and well-being we desire, all the critical elements of life can be realized first through the power of vision.

This book was created and designed to help you harness this power by encouraging you to write and display your visions, keep it before you continually, and intentionally take steps every day to work in cooperation with God's plan and purpose for your life to bring your God-given visions to fruition. Use this book to dream and envision BIG things. Make BOLD and CALCULATED moves as you plan your next steps. Finally, have UNWAVERING faith that your hopes, dreams, and God-ordained visions will become your reality. It's absolutely possible. You can do it!

THE PURPOSE OF THIS JOURNAL-PLANNER

●●●

What You Should Know About This Resource

When you know why something was created, that something can better serve you. This book is all about helping you stay focused on your God-given visions so that you don't lose sight of them. This book isn't meant to make your visions, dreams, and desires into idols in your life, but to encourage you not to neglect God's overall vision and dream for you, which is summed up in Jeremiah 29:11 (KJV):

> For I know the thoughts that I think toward you,
> saith the Lord, thoughts of peace, and not of evil,
> to give you an expected end.

It is God's desire to give you a beautiful, fulfilling life full of peace, love, and prosperity. Will you dare to envision what He sees for you?

Here is something to think about.

There are two ways to execute a vision:

Kill it, by doing nothing,

--or--

Carry it out to completion.

How will you choose to execute your God-given visions?

INSTRUCTIONS

●●●

How To Use This Resource

This resource was crafted to provide a framework for you to succeed. Each section was specially designed to lead and coach you to realizing your God-given visions, by first clarifying and making them plain. Then once that's done, you are encouraged to take the necessary steps to see your visions fully executed by doing what you can do and letting God handle the rest. In order for that to be accomplished, you have to be fully engaged and intentional when using this resource. The following instructions will walk you through how to use each section.

Calendar Section

Use this section to track & note important dates.

Vision Board Section

Use this section to make the vision plain for seven important categories of your life noted in this resource. Select images and text that represent what you envision.

My Next Step Strategy Section

This section features several vital components to help you maintain your focus and keep the vision for each category of your life before you.

A. My Next Steps - Use this section every day to chart out the steps you could take to move you closer to what you envisioned. Remember, just one step a day moves you forward.

B. Projects & To-Do List - This section also helps you plan for weekly projects and provides space for your weekly *To-Do List*. Remember, vision fulfillment starts with being intentional.

C. Spiritual Empowerment - This section was designed to enrich your spiritual development as it relates to your God-given visions. Building a solid relationship with, and staying connected to, the vision-giver is important for seeing all your visions come to fruition. In this section, you will find space where you can note:

- Prayer requests & concerns
- Daily Bible Reading Plan
- Scriptures that speak to me
- Spiritual Downloads
- Divine Expectations & Praise Report
- My Weekly "I AM" and "I WILL" Statements*

* These statements, when crafted in alignment with God's Word, affirm who you are in Him and build your faith on the journey to vision and destiny fulfillment.

Next Step Strategy Section (continued)

The goal for this journal-planner is for you to use this section every day of each week during the year. Doing so, will help you keep your visions before you so you don't lose focus.

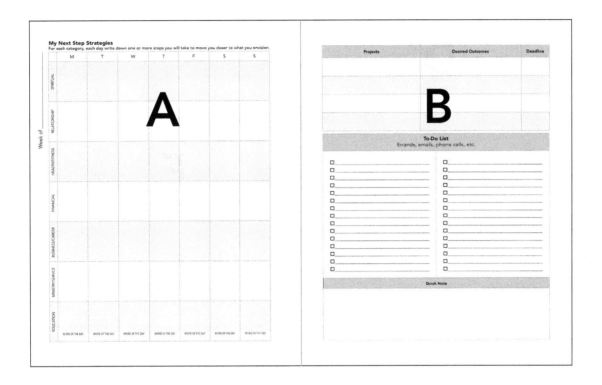

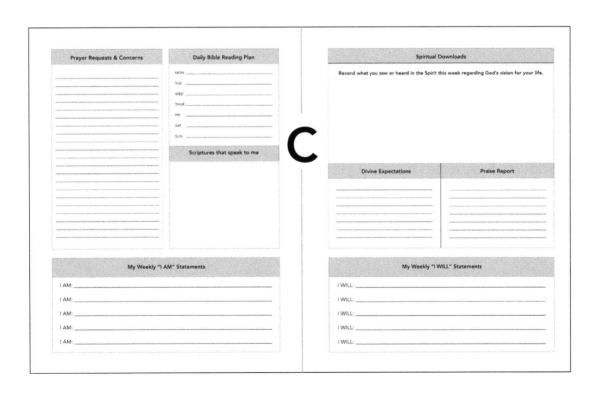

Execute the Vision: My Major Projects for the Year

Use this section to flesh out and work through your specific vision projects during the year. To stay proactive, establish project goals and see them through to completion.

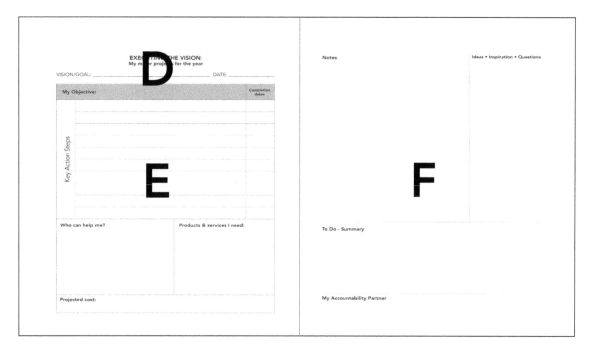

This section helps you pinpoint your vision/goal and allows you to note the start date. These specially designed pages feature the following:

D. My Objective - Use this space to clarify from the start what your main objective will be for this vision.

E. Key Action Steps - This space helps you map out actionable steps you will take and allows you to set and note completion deadlines. Setting deadlines will allow you to gain the upper hand over procrastination and passivity. This worksheet also includes the following:

- Who can help me?
- Products & services I need
- Projected cost

F. Notes, Ideas, Inspiration, Questions - These spaces were designed to allow you to note important milestones when executing your vision. They include:

- Notes
- Ideas, inspiration, questions*
- To-do summary
- My accountability partner

* As you execute your vision, tons of ideas may flood your mind. Be sure to write down what comes. You may or may not use what's flowing when executing the particular vision you're working on, but what comes to you is worth writing down when the download is received.

Also, asking the right questions often leads to the right answers and major breakthroughs. So don't discount asking questions and even questioning your ideas. Finally, be sure to summarize your plans, and find an accountability partner to help you stay on track and complete what you started. This is key to your success, especially if you have trouble sticking to your goals.

My Monthly Finance Tracker

Having a good handle on your money is critical to vision fulfillment. You have to know your financial situation and save to reach your vision goals. Use this worksheet every month to work out your budget and savings plans. A disciplined financial life can open doors to new possibilities.

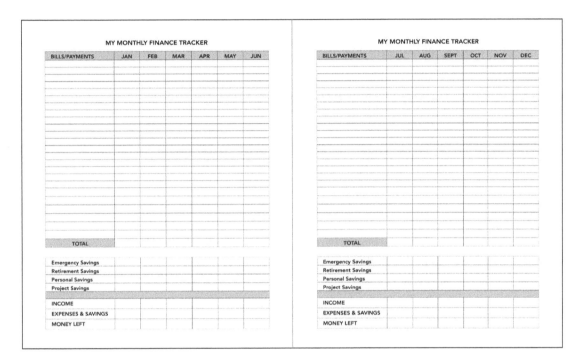

Enrichment & Entertainment

On your journey to vision fulfillment, staying enriched and setting aside time for entertainment is necessary. Leaving no time for growing intellectually, and constantly being engaged in an "all work and no play" mode, will undoubtedly lead to being left behind and ultimately, burnout. To avoid this, use this section to plan the following:

- Books to read
- Movies & documentaries to watch
- What would I do if I had no limitations*
- Courses to take

* Use this space to pull out all the stops and dream BIG! Even dare to dream about things that require a little risk. Don't let your current situation, negative events of the past, or the negative things people have said stop you from listing what's in your heart. Vision and dreaming go hand-in-hand. Never stop dreaming.

Enrichment & Entertainment (continued)

You are encouraged to use this worksheet throughout the year. Strategically plan to have fun and enrich yourself. You're worth it.

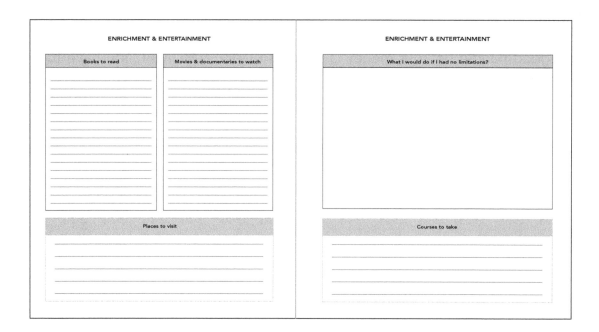

Inspiration & Motivation Section

We all need inspiration and motivation along the way. These two forces help us stay uplifted and encouraged when things get a little tough. Use the worksheet in this section to make a note of the people, things, and events that inspire and motivate you. This vital section includes the following:

- People that inspire me
- Things that inspire me
- Websites to remember
- My Bucket List*
- Conferences & retreats to attend

* Use the *My Bucket List* section to log the special things you want to engage in during the year. Pick things that are new and fresh. Consider a variety of things you have never done before, and plan to make these items a reality in your life. Trying new things and engaging in new settings with new people expands your perspective. This subsequently fuels your ability to envision and dream brighter and bolder outcomes for your life.

Inspiration & Motivation Section (continued)

This is another section where you strategically plan to have fun and also empower yourself. You know what it takes to inspire and motivate you. Defining it on paper brings clarity and gives you something to look forward to.

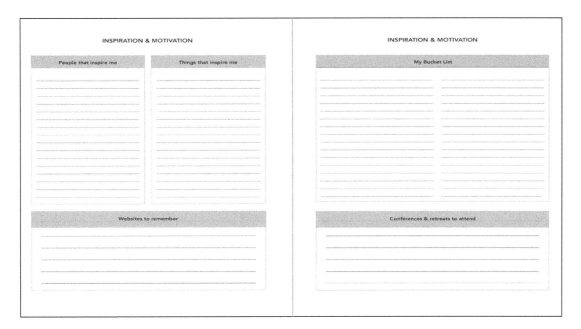

My Gratitude Journal Section

Never underestimate the power of gratitude. With negativity constantly bombarding your mind, it's beneficial to take time to journal about the things you are grateful for. Doing so helps you maintain hope and approach life with a heart of thanksgiving throughout the entire year. Use this section to jot down a few things you are grateful for each day. When this space is filled, consider getting a journal dedicated to tracking what you are grateful for.

SEPTEMBER

Sunday	Monday	Tuesday	Wednesday	Thursday	Friday	Saturday
			1	2	3	4
5	6 Labor Day	7	8	9	10	11 Patriot Day
12 Grandparents' Day	13	14	15	16	17 Citizenship Day	18
19	20	21	22 Fall	23	24	25
26	27	28	29	30		

OCTOBER

Sunday	Monday	Tuesday	Wednesday	Thursday	Friday	Saturday
					1	2
3	4	5	6	7	8	9
10	11 Columbus Day	12	13	14	15 Boss's Day	16
17	18	19	20	21	22	23
24	25	26	27	28	29	30
31 Halloween						

NOVEMBER

2021

Sunday	Monday	Tuesday	Wednesday	Thursday	Friday	Saturday
	1	2	3	4	5	6
7 Daylight Saving Ends (USA & CAN)	8	9	10	11 Veterans Day	12	13
14	15	16	17	18	19	20
21	22	23	24	25 Thanksgiving Day	26 Black Friday	27
28	29 Cyber Monday	30				

DECEMBER

Sunday	Monday	Tuesday	Wednesday	Thursday	Friday	Saturday
			1	2	3	4
5	6	7	8	9	10	11
12	13	14	15	16	17	18
19	20	21	22	23	24 Christmas Eve	25 Christmas
26	27	28	29	30	31 New Year's Eve	

JANUARY

Sunday	Monday	Tuesday	Wednesday	Thursday	Friday	Saturday
						1 New Year's Day
2	3	4	5	6	7	8
9	10	11	12	13	14	15
16	17 Martin Luther King Day (USA)	18	19	20	21	22
23	24	25	26	27	28	29
30	31					

FEBRUARY

Sunday	Monday	Tuesday	Wednesday	Thursday	Friday	Saturday
		1	2 Groundhog Day	3	4	5
6	7	8	9	10	11	12 Lincoln's Birthday
13	14 Valentine's Day	15	16	17	18	19
20	21 Presidents' Day (USA	22	23	24	25	26
27	28					

MARCH

Sunday	Monday	Tuesday	Wednesday	Thursday	Friday	Saturday
		1	2	3	4	5
6	7	8	9	10	11	12
13 Daylight Saving Starts (USA & CAN)	14	15	16	17 St. Patrick's Day (USA)	18	19
20 Spring starts	21	22	23	24	25	26
27	28	29	30	31		

APRIL

Sunday	Monday	Tuesday	Wednesday	Thursday	Friday	Saturday
					1 April Fool's Day	2
3	4	5	6	7	8	9
10	11	12	13	14	15 Good Friday	16
17 Easter Sunday	18	19	20	21	22 Earth Day	23
24	25	26	27	28	29	30

MAY

Sunday	Monday	Tuesday	Wednesday	Thursday	Friday	Saturday
1	2	3	4	5 Cinco de Mayo	6	7
8 Mother's Day	9	10	11	12	13	14
15	16	17	18	19	20	21 Armed Forces Day
22	23	24	25	26	27	28
29	30 Memorial Day	31				

JUNE

Sunday	Monday	Tuesday	Wednesday	Thursday	Friday	Saturday
			1	2	3	4
5 Pentecost	6	7	8	9	10	11
12	13	14 Flag Day	15	16	17	18
19 Father's Day Juneteenth (USA)	20 Juneteenth (USA) Observed	21	22	23	24	25
26	27	28	29	30		

JULY

Sunday	Monday	Tuesday	Wednesday	Thursday	Friday	Saturday
					1	2
3	4 Independence Day	5	6	7	8	9
10	11	12	13	14	15	16
17	18	19	20	21	22	23
24 Parents' Day	25	26	27	28	29	30
31						

AUGUST

Sunday	Monday	Tuesday	Wednesday	Thursday	Friday	Saturday
	1	2	3	4	5	6
7 Friendship Day	8	9	10	11	12	13
14	15	16	17	18	19	20
21	22	23	24	25	26 Women's Equality Day	27
28	29	30	31			

SEPTEMBER

Sunday	Monday	Tuesday	Wednesday	Thursday	Friday	Saturday
				1	2	3
4	5 Labor Day	6	7	8	9	10
11 Patriot Day Grandparents' Day	12	13	14	15	16	17
18	19	20	21	22	23 Native American Day	24
25	26	27	28	29	30	

OCTOBER

Sunday	Monday	Tuesday	Wednesday	Thursday	Friday	Saturday
						1
2	3	4	5	6	7	8
9	10 Columbus Day	11	12	13	14	15
16	17 Boss's Day	18	19	20	21	22
23	24	25	26	27	28	29
30	31 Halloween					

NOVEMBER

Sunday	Monday	Tuesday	Wednesday	Thursday	Friday	Saturday
		1	2	3	4	5
6 Daylight Saving Ends (USA & CAN)	7	8	9	10	11 Veterans Day	12
13	14	15	16	17	18	19
20	21	22	23	24 Thanksgiving Day	25 Black Friday	26
27	28 Cyber Monday	29	30			

DECEMBER

Sunday	Monday	Tuesday	Wednesday	Thursday	Friday	Saturday
				1	2	3
4	5	6	7	8	9	10
11	12	13	14	15	16	17
18	19	20	21	22	23	24 Christmas Eve
25 Christmas	26	27	28	29	30	31 New Year's Eve

THEN THE LORD
ANSWERED ME
AND SAID:
"WRITE
THE VISION
AND MAKE
IT PLAIN ON
TABLETS,
THAT HE MAY RUN
WHO READS IT.
-HABAKKUK 2:2 (NKJV)

MY VISION BOARDS

Use the space provided below to glue or tape 4 to 5 images that represent what you envision for this part of your life.

Use the space provided below to glue or tape 4 to 5 images that represent what you envision for this part of your life.

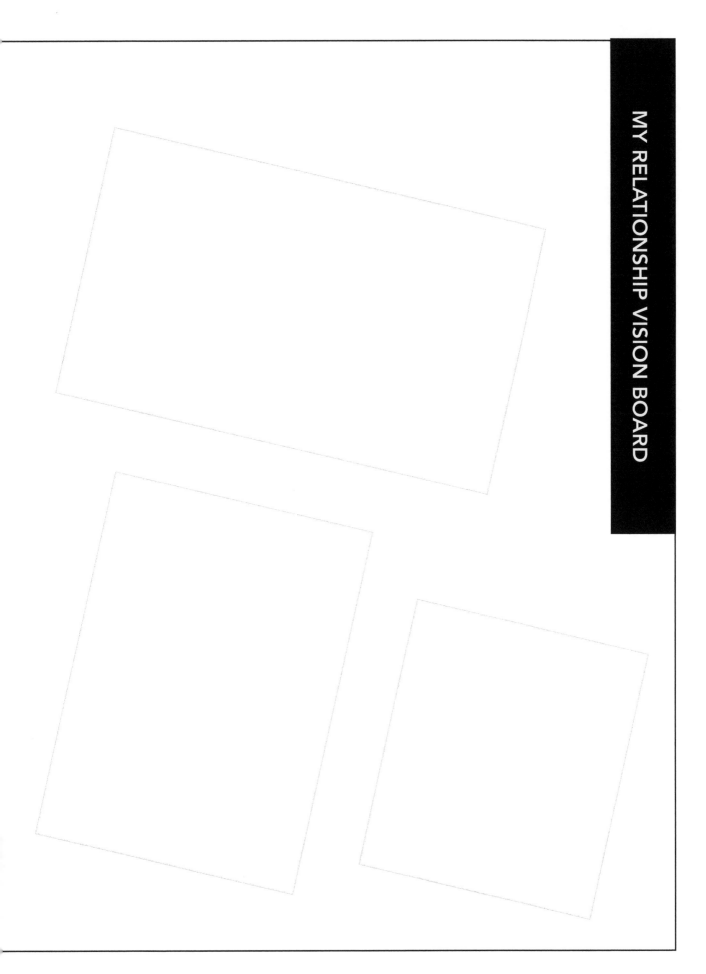

Use the space provided below to glue or tape 4 to 5 images that represent what you envision for this part of your life.

Use the space provided below to glue or tape 4 to 5 images that represent what you envision for this part of your life.

Use the space provided below to glue or tape 4 to 5 images that represent what you envision for this part of your life.

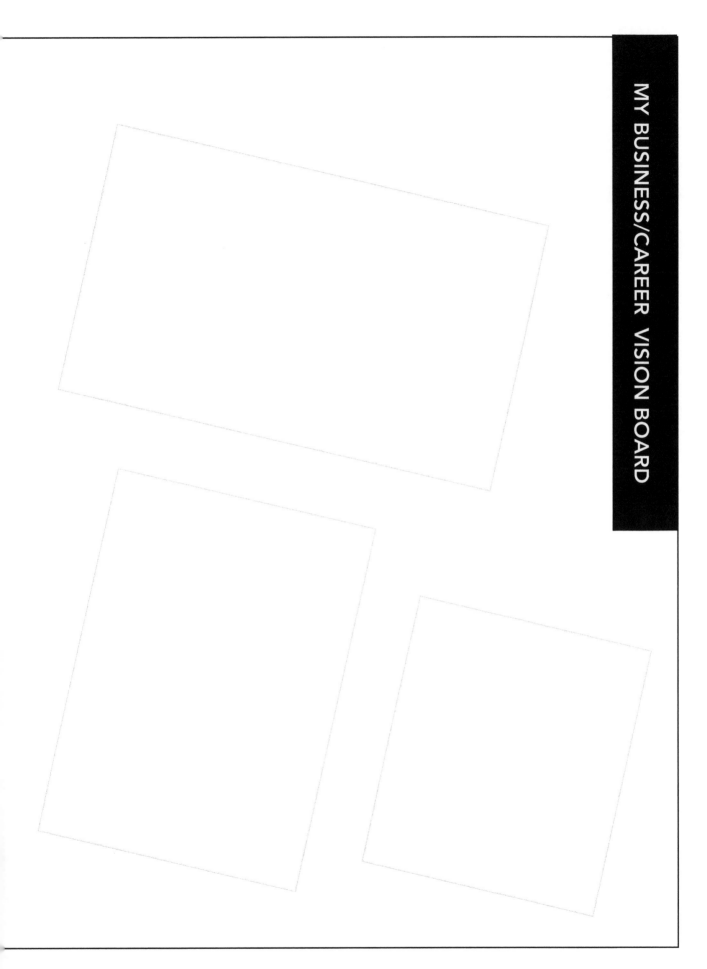

Use the space provided below to glue or tape 4 to 5 images that represent what you envision for this part of your life.

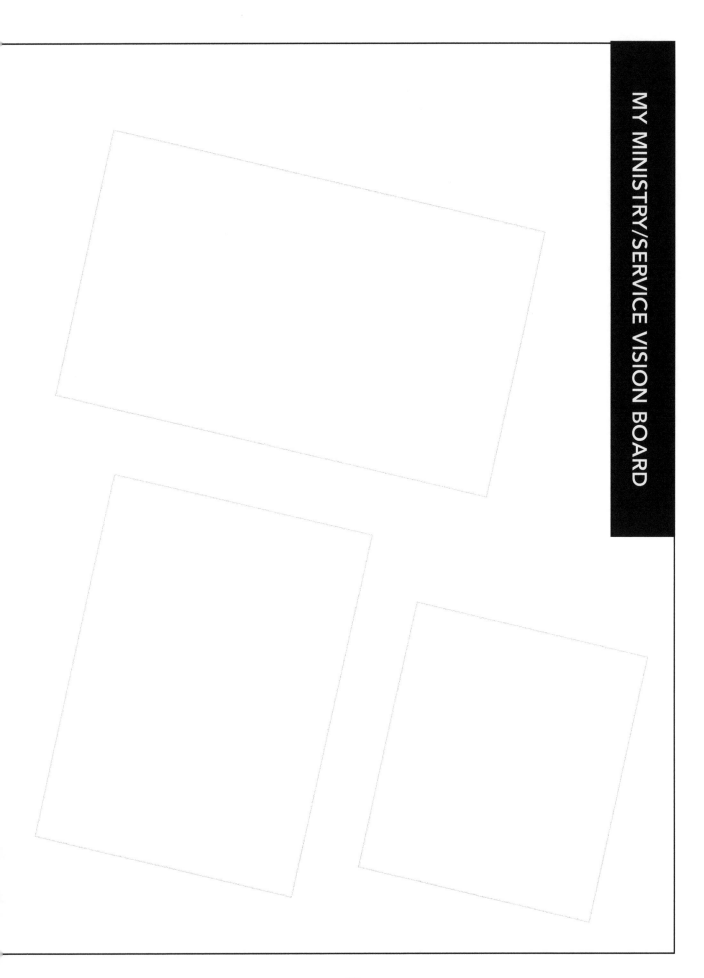

Use the space provided below to glue or tape 4 to 5 images that represent what you envision for this part of your life.

EVERY STEP YOU TAKE

———————————

BRINGS YOU CLOSER

———————————

TO WHAT YOU ENVISIONED
AND DREAM OF BEING,
HAVING, AND DOING.

MY NEXT STEP STRATEGY

My Next Step Strategy

For each category, each day write down one or more steps you will take to move you closer to what you envision.

	M	T	W	T	F	S	S
SPIRITUAL							
RELATIONSHIP							
HEALTH/FITNESS							
FINANCIAL							
BUSINESS/CAREER							
MINISTRY/SERVICE							
EDUCATION							
	WORD OF THE DAY:	WORD OF THE DAY:	WORD OF THE DAY:	WORD OF THE DAY:	WORD OF THE DAY:	WORD OF THE DAY:	WORD OF THE DAY:

Week of _____

Projects	Desired Outcomes	Deadline

To-Do List
Errands, emails, phone calls, etc.

- ☐ _____
- ☐ _____
- ☐ _____
- ☐ _____
- ☐ _____
- ☐ _____
- ☐ _____
- ☐ _____
- ☐ _____
- ☐ _____
- ☐ _____
- ☐ _____
- ☐ _____
- ☐ _____
- ☐ _____

- ☐ _____
- ☐ _____
- ☐ _____
- ☐ _____
- ☐ _____
- ☐ _____
- ☐ _____
- ☐ _____
- ☐ _____
- ☐ _____
- ☐ _____
- ☐ _____
- ☐ _____
- ☐ _____
- ☐ _____

Quick Note

Prayer Requests & Concerns

_____
_____
_____
_____
_____
_____
_____
_____
_____
_____
_____
_____
_____
_____
_____
_____
_____
_____
_____
_____
_____

Daily Bible Reading Plan

MON _____

TUE _____

WED _____

THUR _____

FRI _____

SAT _____

SUN _____

Scriptures that speak to me

My Weekly "I AM" Statements

I AM: _____

I AM: _____

I AM: _____

I AM: _____

I AM: _____

Spiritual Downloads

Record what you saw or heard in the Spirit this week regarding God's vision for your life.

Divine Expectations	Praise Report
_____	_____
_____	_____
_____	_____
_____	_____
_____	_____
_____	_____
_____	

My Weekly "I WILL" Statements

I WILL: _____

I WILL: _____

I WILL: _____

I WILL: _____

I WILL: _____

My Next Step Strategy

For each category, each day write down one or more steps you will take to move you closer to what you envision.

	M	T	W	T	F	S	S
SPIRITUAL							
RELATIONSHIP							
HEALTH/FITNESS							
FINANCIAL							
BUSINESS/CAREER							
MINISTRY/SERVICE							
EDUCATION							
	WORD OF THE DAY:	WORD OF THE DAY:	WORD OF THE DAY:	WORD OF THE DAY:	WORD OF THE DAY:	WORD OF THE DAY:	WORD OF THE DAY:

Week of _____

Projects	Desired Outcomes	Deadline

To-Do List
Errands, emails, phone calls, etc.

☐ _____
☐ _____
☐ _____
☐ _____
☐ _____
☐ _____
☐ _____
☐ _____
☐ _____
☐ _____
☐ _____
☐ _____
☐ _____
☐ _____
☐ _____

☐ _____
☐ _____
☐ _____
☐ _____
☐ _____
☐ _____
☐ _____
☐ _____
☐ _____
☐ _____
☐ _____
☐ _____
☐ _____
☐ _____
☐ _____

Quick Note

Prayer Requests & Concerns

Daily Bible Reading Plan

MON _____

TUE _____

WED _____

THUR _____

FRI _____

SAT _____

SUN _____

Scriptures that speak to me

My Weekly "I AM" Statements

I AM: _____

I AM: _____

I AM: _____

I AM: _____

I AM: _____

Spiritual Downloads

Record what you saw or heard in the Spirit this week regarding God's vision for your life.

Divine Expectations	Praise Report
_____	_____
_____	_____
_____	_____
_____	_____
_____	_____
_____	_____
_____	_____

My Weekly "I WILL" Statements

I WILL: _____

I WILL: _____

I WILL: _____

I WILL: _____

I WILL: _____

My Next Step Strategy

For each category, each day write down one or more steps you will take to move you closer to what you envision.

Week of _____

	M	T	W	T	F	S	S
SPIRITUAL							
RELATIONSHIP							
HEALTH/FITNESS							
FINANCIAL							
BUSINESS/CAREER							
MINISTRY/SERVICE							
EDUCATION							
	WORD OF THE DAY:	WORD OF THE DAY:	WORD OF THE DAY:	WORD OF THE DAY:	WORD OF THE DAY:	WORD OF THE DAY:	WORD OF THE DAY:

Projects	Desired Outcomes	Deadline

To-Do List
Errands, emails, phone calls, etc.

☐ _____
☐ _____
☐ _____
☐ _____
☐ _____
☐ _____
☐ _____
☐ _____
☐ _____
☐ _____
☐ _____
☐ _____
☐ _____
☐ _____

☐ _____
☐ _____
☐ _____
☐ _____
☐ _____
☐ _____
☐ _____
☐ _____
☐ _____
☐ _____
☐ _____
☐ _____
☐ _____
☐ _____

Quick Note

Prayer Requests & Concerns

_____
_____
_____
_____
_____
_____
_____
_____
_____
_____
_____
_____
_____
_____
_____
_____
_____
_____
_____
_____
_____

Daily Bible Reading Plan

MON _____

TUE _____

WED _____

THUR _____

FRI _____

SAT _____

SUN _____

Scriptures that speak to me

My Weekly "I AM" Statements

I AM: _____

I AM: _____

I AM: _____

I AM: _____

I AM: _____

Spiritual Downloads

Record what you saw or heard in the Spirit this week regarding God's vision for your life.

Divine Expectations	Praise Report
_____	_____
_____	_____
_____	_____
_____	_____
_____	_____
_____	_____
_____	_____

My Weekly "I WILL" Statements

I WILL: _____

I WILL: _____

I WILL: _____

I WILL: _____

I WILL: _____

My Next Step Strategy

For each category, each day write down one or more steps you will take to move you closer to what you envision.

	M	T	W	T	F	S	S
SPIRITUAL							
RELATIONSHIP							
HEALTH/FITNESS							
FINANCIAL							
BUSINESS/CAREER							
MINISTRY/SERVICE							
EDUCATION							
	WORD OF THE DAY:	WORD OF THE DAY:	WORD OF THE DAY:	WORD OF THE DAY:	WORD OF THE DAY:	WORD OF THE DAY:	WORD OF THE DAY:

Week of _____

Projects	Desired Outcomes	Deadline

To-Do List
Errands, emails, phone calls, etc.

- ☐ _____
- ☐ _____
- ☐ _____
- ☐ _____
- ☐ _____
- ☐ _____
- ☐ _____
- ☐ _____
- ☐ _____
- ☐ _____
- ☐ _____
- ☐ _____
- ☐ _____
- ☐ _____
- ☐ _____

- ☐ _____
- ☐ _____
- ☐ _____
- ☐ _____
- ☐ _____
- ☐ _____
- ☐ _____
- ☐ _____
- ☐ _____
- ☐ _____
- ☐ _____
- ☐ _____
- ☐ _____
- ☐ _____
- ☐ _____

Quick Note

Prayer Requests & Concerns

_____
_____
_____
_____
_____
_____
_____
_____
_____
_____
_____
_____
_____
_____
_____
_____
_____
_____
_____
_____
_____

Daily Bible Reading Plan

MON _____

TUE _____

WED _____

THUR _____

FRI _____

SAT _____

SUN _____

Scriptures that speak to me

My Weekly "I AM" Statements

I AM: _____

I AM: _____

I AM: _____

I AM: _____

I AM: _____

Spiritual Downloads

Record what you saw or heard in the Spirit this week regarding God's vision for your life.

Divine Expectations	Praise Report
_____	_____
_____	_____
_____	_____
_____	_____
_____	_____
_____	_____
_____	_____

My Weekly "I WILL" Statements

I WILL: _____

I WILL: _____

I WILL: _____

I WILL: _____

I WILL: _____

My Next Step Strategy

For each category, each day write down one or more steps you will take to move you closer to what you envision.

Week of _____

	M	T	W	T	F	S	S
SPIRITUAL							
RELATIONSHIP							
HEALTH/FITNESS							
FINANCIAL							
BUSINESS/CAREER							
MINISTRY/SERVICE							
EDUCATION	WORD OF THE DAY:	WORD OF THE DAY:	WORD OF THE DAY:	WORD OF THE DAY:	WORD OF THE DAY:	WORD OF THE DAY:	WORD OF THE DAY:

Projects	Desired Outcomes	Deadline

To-Do List
Errands, emails, phone calls, etc.

- ☐ _____
- ☐ _____
- ☐ _____
- ☐ _____
- ☐ _____
- ☐ _____
- ☐ _____
- ☐ _____
- ☐ _____
- ☐ _____
- ☐ _____
- ☐ _____
- ☐ _____
- ☐ _____
- ☐ _____

- ☐ _____
- ☐ _____
- ☐ _____
- ☐ _____
- ☐ _____
- ☐ _____
- ☐ _____
- ☐ _____
- ☐ _____
- ☐ _____
- ☐ _____
- ☐ _____
- ☐ _____
- ☐ _____
- ☐ _____

Quick Note

Prayer Requests & Concerns

_____
_____
_____
_____
_____
_____
_____
_____
_____
_____
_____
_____
_____
_____
_____
_____
_____
_____
_____

Daily Bible Reading Plan

MON _____

TUE _____

WED _____

THUR _____

FRI _____

SAT _____

SUN _____

Scriptures that speak to me

My Weekly "I AM" Statements

I AM: _____

I AM: _____

I AM: _____

I AM: _____

I AM: _____

Spiritual Downloads

Record what you saw or heard in the Spirit this week regarding God's vision for your life.

Divine Expectations	Praise Report
_____	_____
_____	_____
_____	_____
_____	_____
_____	_____
_____	_____
_____	_____

My Weekly "I WILL" Statements

I WILL: _____

I WILL: _____

I WILL: _____

I WILL: _____

I WILL: _____

My Next Step Strategy

For each category, each day write down one or more steps you will take to move you closer to what you envision.

Week of _____

	M	T	W	T	F	S	S
SPIRITUAL							
RELATIONSHIP							
HEALTH/FITNESS							
FINANCIAL							
BUSINESS/CAREER							
MINISTRY/SERVICE							
EDUCATION							
	WORD OF THE DAY:	WORD OF THE DAY:	WORD OF THE DAY:	WORD OF THE DAY:	WORD OF THE DAY:	WORD OF THE DAY:	WORD OF THE DAY:

Projects	Desired Outcomes	Deadline

To-Do List
Errands, emails, phone calls, etc.

☐ _____
☐ _____
☐ _____
☐ _____
☐ _____
☐ _____
☐ _____
☐ _____
☐ _____
☐ _____
☐ _____
☐ _____
☐ _____
☐ _____

☐ _____
☐ _____
☐ _____
☐ _____
☐ _____
☐ _____
☐ _____
☐ _____
☐ _____
☐ _____
☐ _____
☐ _____
☐ _____
☐ _____

Quick Note

Prayer Requests & Concerns

_____
_____
_____
_____
_____
_____
_____
_____
_____
_____
_____
_____
_____
_____
_____
_____
_____
_____
_____
_____
_____

Daily Bible Reading Plan

MON _____

TUE _____

WED _____

THUR _____

FRI _____

SAT _____

SUN _____

Scriptures that speak to me

My Weekly "I AM" Statements

I AM: _____

I AM: _____

I AM: _____

I AM: _____

I AM: _____

Spiritual Downloads

Record what you saw or heard in the Spirit this week regarding God's vision for your life.

Divine Expectations	Praise Report
_____	_____
_____	_____
_____	_____
_____	_____
_____	_____
_____	_____
_____	_____

My Weekly "I WILL" Statements

I WILL: _____

I WILL: _____

I WILL: _____

I WILL: _____

I WILL: _____

My Next Step Strategy

For each category, each day write down one or more steps you will take to move you closer to what you envision.

Week of _____	M	T	W	T	F	S	S
SPIRITUAL							
RELATIONSHIP							
HEALTH/FITNESS							
FINANCIAL							
BUSINESS/CAREER							
MINISTRY/SERVICE							
EDUCATION							
	WORD OF THE DAY:	WORD OF THE DAY:	WORD OF THE DAY:	WORD OF THE DAY:	WORD OF THE DAY:	WORD OF THE DAY:	WORD OF THE DAY:

Projects	Desired Outcomes	Deadline

To-Do List
Errands, emails, phone calls, etc.

☐ _____
☐ _____
☐ _____
☐ _____
☐ _____
☐ _____
☐ _____
☐ _____
☐ _____
☐ _____
☐ _____
☐ _____
☐ _____
☐ _____

☐ _____
☐ _____
☐ _____
☐ _____
☐ _____
☐ _____
☐ _____
☐ _____
☐ _____
☐ _____
☐ _____
☐ _____
☐ _____
☐ _____

Quick Note

Prayer Requests & Concerns

_____
_____
_____
_____
_____
_____
_____
_____
_____
_____
_____
_____
_____
_____
_____
_____
_____
_____

Daily Bible Reading Plan

MON _____

TUE _____

WED _____

THUR _____

FRI _____

SAT _____

SUN _____

Scriptures that speak to me

My Weekly "I AM" Statements

I AM: _____

I AM: _____

I AM: _____

I AM: _____

I AM: _____

Spiritual Downloads

Record what you saw or heard in the Spirit this week regarding God's vision for your life.

Divine Expectations	Praise Report
_____	_____
_____	_____
_____	_____
_____	_____
_____	_____
_____	_____
_____	_____

My Weekly "I WILL" Statements

I WILL: _____

I WILL: _____

I WILL: _____

I WILL: _____

I WILL: _____

My Next Step Strategy

For each category, each day write down one or more steps you will take to move you closer to what you envision.

Week of _____

	M	T	W	T	F	S	S
SPIRITUAL							
RELATIONSHIP							
HEALTH/FITNESS							
FINANCIAL							
BUSINESS/CAREER							
MINISTRY/SERVICE							
EDUCATION							
	WORD OF THE DAY:	WORD OF THE DAY:	WORD OF THE DAY:	WORD OF THE DAY:	WORD OF THE DAY:	WORD OF THE DAY:	WORD OF THE DAY:

Projects	Desired Outcomes	Deadline

To-Do List
Errands, emails, phone calls, etc.

☐ _____
☐ _____
☐ _____
☐ _____
☐ _____
☐ _____
☐ _____
☐ _____
☐ _____
☐ _____
☐ _____
☐ _____
☐ _____
☐ _____
☐ _____

☐ _____
☐ _____
☐ _____
☐ _____
☐ _____
☐ _____
☐ _____
☐ _____
☐ _____
☐ _____
☐ _____
☐ _____
☐ _____
☐ _____
☐ _____

Quick Note

Prayer Requests & Concerns

_____
_____
_____
_____
_____
_____
_____
_____
_____
_____
_____
_____
_____
_____
_____
_____
_____
_____
_____
_____
_____

Daily Bible Reading Plan

MON _____

TUE _____

WED _____

THUR _____

FRI _____

SAT _____

SUN _____

Scriptures that speak to me

My Weekly "I AM" Statements

I AM: _____

I AM: _____

I AM: _____

I AM: _____

I AM: _____

Spiritual Downloads

Record what you saw or heard in the Spirit this week regarding God's vision for your life.

Divine Expectations	Praise Report
_____	_____
_____	_____
_____	_____
_____	_____
_____	_____
_____	_____
_____	_____

My Weekly "I WILL" Statements

I WILL: _____

I WILL: _____

I WILL: _____

I WILL: _____

I WILL: _____

My Next Step Strategy

For each category, each day write down one or more steps you will take to move you closer to what you envision.

Week of _____

	M	T	W	T	F	S	S
SPIRITUAL							
RELATIONSHIP							
HEALTH/FITNESS							
FINANCIAL							
BUSINESS/CAREER							
MINISTRY/SERVICE							
EDUCATION							
	WORD OF THE DAY:	WORD OF THE DAY:	WORD OF THE DAY:	WORD OF THE DAY:	WORD OF THE DAY:	WORD OF THE DAY:	WORD OF THE DAY:

Projects	Desired Outcomes	Deadline

To-Do List
Errands, emails, phone calls, etc.

☐ _____
☐ _____
☐ _____
☐ _____
☐ _____
☐ _____
☐ _____
☐ _____
☐ _____
☐ _____
☐ _____
☐ _____
☐ _____
☐ _____
☐ _____

☐ _____
☐ _____
☐ _____
☐ _____
☐ _____
☐ _____
☐ _____
☐ _____
☐ _____
☐ _____
☐ _____
☐ _____
☐ _____
☐ _____
☐ _____

Quick Note

Prayer Requests & Concerns

_____
_____
_____
_____
_____
_____
_____
_____
_____
_____
_____
_____
_____
_____
_____
_____
_____
_____
_____

Daily Bible Reading Plan

MON _____

TUE _____

WED _____

THUR _____

FRI _____

SAT _____

SUN _____

Scriptures that speak to me

My Weekly "I AM" Statements

I AM: _____

I AM: _____

I AM: _____

I AM: _____

I AM: _____

Spiritual Downloads

Record what you saw or heard in the Spirit this week regarding God's vision for your life.

Divine Expectations

_____
_____
_____
_____
_____
_____
_____

Praise Report

_____
_____
_____
_____
_____
_____
_____

My Weekly "I WILL" Statements

I WILL: _____

I WILL: _____

I WILL: _____

I WILL: _____

I WILL: _____

My Next Step Strategy
For each category, each day write down one or more steps you will take to move you closer to what you envision.

	M	T	W	T	F	S	S
SPIRITUAL							
RELATIONSHIP							
HEALTH/FITNESS							
FINANCIAL							
BUSINESS/CAREER							
MINISTRY/SERVICE							
EDUCATION							
	WORD OF THE DAY:	WORD OF THE DAY:	WORD OF THE DAY:	WORD OF THE DAY:	WORD OF THE DAY:	WORD OF THE DAY:	WORD OF THE DAY:

Week of ____

Projects	Desired Outcomes	Deadline

To-Do List
Errands, emails, phone calls, etc.

☐ _____
☐ _____
☐ _____
☐ _____
☐ _____
☐ _____
☐ _____
☐ _____
☐ _____
☐ _____
☐ _____
☐ _____
☐ _____
☐ _____

☐ _____
☐ _____
☐ _____
☐ _____
☐ _____
☐ _____
☐ _____
☐ _____
☐ _____
☐ _____
☐ _____
☐ _____
☐ _____
☐ _____

Quick Note

Prayer Requests & Concerns

_____
_____
_____
_____
_____
_____
_____
_____
_____
_____
_____
_____
_____
_____
_____
_____
_____
_____
_____
_____

Daily Bible Reading Plan

MON _____

TUE _____

WED _____

THUR _____

FRI _____

SAT _____

SUN _____

Scriptures that speak to me

My Weekly "I AM" Statements

I AM: _____

I AM: _____

I AM: _____

I AM: _____

I AM: _____

Spiritual Downloads

Record what you saw or heard in the Spirit this week regarding God's vision for your life.

Divine Expectations	Praise Report
_____	_____
_____	_____
_____	_____
_____	_____
_____	_____
_____	_____
_____	_____

My Weekly "I WILL" Statements

I WILL: _____

I WILL: _____

I WILL: _____

I WILL: _____

I WILL: _____

My Next Step Strategy

For each category, each day write down one or more steps you will take to move you closer to what you envision.

Week of _____

	M	T	W	T	F	S	S
SPIRITUAL							
RELATIONSHIP							
HEALTH/FITNESS							
FINANCIAL							
BUSINESS/CAREER							
MINISTRY/SERVICE							
EDUCATION							
	WORD OF THE DAY:	WORD OF THE DAY:	WORD OF THE DAY:	WORD OF THE DAY:	WORD OF THE DAY:	WORD OF THE DAY:	WORD OF THE DAY:

Projects	Desired Outcomes	Deadline

To-Do List
Errands, emails, phone calls, etc.

☐ _____
☐ _____
☐ _____
☐ _____
☐ _____
☐ _____
☐ _____
☐ _____
☐ _____
☐ _____
☐ _____
☐ _____
☐ _____
☐ _____
☐ _____

☐ _____
☐ _____
☐ _____
☐ _____
☐ _____
☐ _____
☐ _____
☐ _____
☐ _____
☐ _____
☐ _____
☐ _____
☐ _____
☐ _____
☐ _____

Quick Note

Prayer Requests & Concerns

_____
_____
_____
_____
_____
_____
_____
_____
_____
_____
_____
_____
_____
_____
_____
_____
_____
_____
_____
_____

Daily Bible Reading Plan

MON _____

TUE _____

WED _____

THUR _____

FRI _____

SAT _____

SUN _____

Scriptures that speak to me

My Weekly "I AM" Statements

I AM: _____

I AM: _____

I AM: _____

I AM: _____

I AM: _____

Spiritual Downloads

Record what you saw or heard in the Spirit this week regarding God's vision for your life.

Divine Expectations	Praise Report
_____	_____
_____	_____
_____	_____
_____	_____
_____	_____
_____	_____
_____	_____

My Weekly "I WILL" Statements

I WILL: _____

I WILL: _____

I WILL: _____

I WILL: _____

I WILL: _____

My Next Step Strategy

For each category, each day write down one or more steps you will take to move you closer to what you envision.

Week of _____

	M	T	W	T	F	S	S
SPIRITUAL							
RELATIONSHIP							
HEALTH/FITNESS							
FINANCIAL							
BUSINESS/CAREER							
MINISTRY/SERVICE							
EDUCATION							
	WORD OF THE DAY:	WORD OF THE DAY:	WORD OF THE DAY:	WORD OF THE DAY:	WORD OF THE DAY:	WORD OF THE DAY:	WORD OF THE DAY:

Projects	Desired Outcomes	Deadline

To-Do List
Errands, emails, phone calls, etc.

☐ _____
☐ _____
☐ _____
☐ _____
☐ _____
☐ _____
☐ _____
☐ _____
☐ _____
☐ _____
☐ _____
☐ _____
☐ _____
☐ _____

☐ _____
☐ _____
☐ _____
☐ _____
☐ _____
☐ _____
☐ _____
☐ _____
☐ _____
☐ _____
☐ _____
☐ _____
☐ _____
☐ _____

Quick Note

Prayer Requests & Concerns

_____
_____
_____
_____
_____
_____
_____
_____
_____
_____
_____
_____
_____
_____
_____
_____
_____
_____
_____
_____
_____

Daily Bible Reading Plan

MON _____

TUE _____

WED _____

THUR _____

FRI _____

SAT _____

SUN _____

Scriptures that speak to me

My Weekly "I AM" Statements

I AM: _____

I AM: _____

I AM: _____

I AM: _____

I AM: _____

Spiritual Downloads

Record what you saw or heard in the Spirit this week regarding God's vision for your life.

Divine Expectations	Praise Report
_____	_____
_____	_____
_____	_____
_____	_____
_____	_____
_____	_____
_____	_____

My Weekly "I WILL" Statements

I WILL: _____

I WILL: _____

I WILL: _____

I WILL: _____

I WILL: _____

My Next Step Strategy

For each category, each day write down one or more steps you will take to move you closer to what you envision.

Week of _____

	M	T	W	T	F	S	S
SPIRITUAL							
RELATIONSHIP							
HEALTH/FITNESS							
FINANCIAL							
BUSINESS/CAREER							
MINISTRY/SERVICE							
EDUCATION							
	WORD OF THE DAY:	WORD OF THE DAY:	WORD OF THE DAY:	WORD OF THE DAY:	WORD OF THE DAY:	WORD OF THE DAY:	WORD OF THE DAY:

Projects	Desired Outcomes	Deadline

To-Do List
Errands, emails, phone calls, etc.

- ☐ _____
- ☐ _____
- ☐ _____
- ☐ _____
- ☐ _____
- ☐ _____
- ☐ _____
- ☐ _____
- ☐ _____
- ☐ _____
- ☐ _____
- ☐ _____
- ☐ _____
- ☐ _____
- ☐ _____

- ☐ _____
- ☐ _____
- ☐ _____
- ☐ _____
- ☐ _____
- ☐ _____
- ☐ _____
- ☐ _____
- ☐ _____
- ☐ _____
- ☐ _____
- ☐ _____
- ☐ _____
- ☐ _____

Quick Note

Prayer Requests & Concerns

_____
_____
_____
_____
_____
_____
_____
_____
_____
_____
_____
_____
_____
_____
_____
_____
_____
_____
_____
_____

Daily Bible Reading Plan

MON _____

TUE _____

WED _____

THUR _____

FRI _____

SAT _____

SUN _____

Scriptures that speak to me

My Weekly "I AM" Statements

I AM: _____

I AM: _____

I AM: _____

I AM: _____

I AM: _____

Spiritual Downloads

Record what you saw or heard in the Spirit this week regarding God's vision for your life.

Divine Expectations	Praise Report
_____	_____
_____	_____
_____	_____
_____	_____
_____	_____
_____	_____
_____	_____

My Weekly "I WILL" Statements

I WILL: _____

I WILL: _____

I WILL: _____

I WILL: _____

I WILL: _____

My Next Step Strategy

For each category, each day write down one or more steps you will take to move you closer to what you envision.

Week of ___	M	T	W	T	F	S	S
SPIRITUAL							
RELATIONSHIP							
HEALTH/FITNESS							
FINANCIAL							
BUSINESS/CAREER							
MINISTRY/SERVICE							
EDUCATION							
	WORD OF THE DAY:	WORD OF THE DAY:	WORD OF THE DAY:	WORD OF THE DAY:	WORD OF THE DAY:	WORD OF THE DAY:	WORD OF THE DAY:

Projects	Desired Outcomes	Deadline

To-Do List
Errands, emails, phone calls, etc.

☐ _____
☐ _____
☐ _____
☐ _____
☐ _____
☐ _____
☐ _____
☐ _____
☐ _____
☐ _____
☐ _____
☐ _____
☐ _____

☐ _____
☐ _____
☐ _____
☐ _____
☐ _____
☐ _____
☐ _____
☐ _____
☐ _____
☐ _____
☐ _____
☐ _____
☐ _____

Quick Note

Prayer Requests & Concerns

_____
_____
_____
_____
_____
_____
_____
_____
_____
_____
_____
_____
_____
_____
_____
_____
_____
_____
_____
_____

Daily Bible Reading Plan

MON _____

TUE _____

WED _____

THUR _____

FRI _____

SAT _____

SUN _____

Scriptures that speak to me

My Weekly "I AM" Statements

I AM: _____

I AM: _____

I AM: _____

I AM: _____

I AM: _____

Spiritual Downloads

Record what you saw or heard in the Spirit this week regarding God's vision for your life.

Divine Expectations	Praise Report
_____	_____
_____	_____
_____	_____
_____	_____
_____	_____
_____	_____
_____	_____

My Weekly "I WILL" Statements

I WILL: _____

I WILL: _____

I WILL: _____

I WILL: _____

I WILL: _____

My Next Step Strategy

For each category, each day write down one or more steps you will take to move you closer to what you envision.

Week of _____

	M	T	W	T	F	S	S
SPIRITUAL							
RELATIONSHIP							
HEALTH/FITNESS							
FINANCIAL							
BUSINESS/CAREER							
MINISTRY/SERVICE							
EDUCATION							
	WORD OF THE DAY:	WORD OF THE DAY:	WORD OF THE DAY:	WORD OF THE DAY:	WORD OF THE DAY:	WORD OF THE DAY:	WORD OF THE DAY:

Projects	Desired Outcomes	Deadline

To-Do List
Errands, emails, phone calls, etc.

- ☐ _____
- ☐ _____
- ☐ _____
- ☐ _____
- ☐ _____
- ☐ _____
- ☐ _____
- ☐ _____
- ☐ _____
- ☐ _____
- ☐ _____
- ☐ _____
- ☐ _____
- ☐ _____

- ☐ _____
- ☐ _____
- ☐ _____
- ☐ _____
- ☐ _____
- ☐ _____
- ☐ _____
- ☐ _____
- ☐ _____
- ☐ _____
- ☐ _____
- ☐ _____
- ☐ _____
- ☐ _____

Quick Note

Prayer Requests & Concerns

_____
_____
_____
_____
_____
_____
_____
_____
_____
_____
_____
_____
_____
_____
_____
_____
_____
_____
_____
_____
_____
_____

Daily Bible Reading Plan

MON _____

TUE _____

WED _____

THUR _____

FRI _____

SAT _____

SUN _____

Scriptures that speak to me

My Weekly "I AM" Statements

I AM: _____

I AM: _____

I AM: _____

I AM: _____

I AM: _____

Spiritual Downloads

Record what you saw or heard in the Spirit this week regarding God's vision for your life.

Divine Expectations	Praise Report
_____	_____
_____	_____
_____	_____
_____	_____
_____	_____
_____	_____

My Weekly "I WILL" Statements

I WILL: _____

I WILL: _____

I WILL: _____

I WILL: _____

I WILL: _____

My Next Step Strategy
For each category, each day write down one or more steps you will take to move you closer to what you envision.

Week of _____

	M	T	W	T	F	S	S
SPIRITUAL							
RELATIONSHIP							
HEALTH/FITNESS							
FINANCIAL							
BUSINESS/CAREER							
MINISTRY/SERVICE							
EDUCATION							
	WORD OF THE DAY:	WORD OF THE DAY:	WORD OF THE DAY:	WORD OF THE DAY:	WORD OF THE DAY:	WORD OF THE DAY:	WORD OF THE DAY:

Projects	Desired Outcomes	Deadline

To-Do List
Errands, emails, phone calls, etc.

☐ _____
☐ _____
☐ _____
☐ _____
☐ _____
☐ _____
☐ _____
☐ _____
☐ _____
☐ _____
☐ _____
☐ _____
☐ _____
☐ _____
☐ _____

☐ _____
☐ _____
☐ _____
☐ _____
☐ _____
☐ _____
☐ _____
☐ _____
☐ _____
☐ _____
☐ _____
☐ _____
☐ _____
☐ _____

Quick Note

Prayer Requests & Concerns

_____
_____
_____
_____
_____
_____
_____
_____
_____
_____
_____
_____
_____
_____
_____
_____
_____
_____
_____
_____
_____
_____

Daily Bible Reading Plan

MON _____

TUE _____

WED _____

THUR _____

FRI _____

SAT _____

SUN _____

Scriptures that speak to me

My Weekly "I AM" Statements

I AM: _____

I AM: _____

I AM: _____

I AM: _____

I AM: _____

Spiritual Downloads

Record what you saw or heard in the Spirit this week regarding God's vision for your life.

Divine Expectations	Praise Report
_____	_____
_____	_____
_____	_____
_____	_____
_____	_____
_____	_____
_____	_____

My Weekly "I WILL" Statements

I WILL: _____

I WILL: _____

I WILL: _____

I WILL: _____

I WILL: _____

My Next Step Strategy

For each category, each day write down one or more steps you will take to move you closer to what you envision.

Week of _____

	M	T	W	T	F	S	S
SPIRITUAL							
RELATIONSHIP							
HEALTH/FITNESS							
FINANCIAL							
BUSINESS/CAREER							
MINISTRY/SERVICE							
EDUCATION							
	WORD OF THE DAY:	WORD OF THE DAY:	WORD OF THE DAY:	WORD OF THE DAY:	WORD OF THE DAY:	WORD OF THE DAY:	WORD OF THE DAY:

Projects	Desired Outcomes	Deadline

To-Do List
Errands, emails, phone calls, etc.

☐ _____
☐ _____
☐ _____
☐ _____
☐ _____
☐ _____
☐ _____
☐ _____
☐ _____
☐ _____
☐ _____
☐ _____
☐ _____
☐ _____
☐ _____

☐ _____
☐ _____
☐ _____
☐ _____
☐ _____
☐ _____
☐ _____
☐ _____
☐ _____
☐ _____
☐ _____
☐ _____
☐ _____
☐ _____
☐ _____

Quick Note

Prayer Requests & Concerns

_____
_____
_____
_____
_____
_____
_____
_____
_____
_____
_____
_____
_____
_____
_____
_____
_____
_____
_____
_____

Daily Bible Reading Plan

MON _____

TUE _____

WED _____

THUR _____

FRI _____

SAT _____

SUN _____

Scriptures that speak to me

My Weekly "I AM" Statements

I AM: _____

I AM: _____

I AM: _____

I AM: _____

I AM: _____

Spiritual Downloads

Record what you saw or heard in the Spirit this week regarding God's vision for your life.

Divine Expectations	Praise Report
_____	_____
_____	_____
_____	_____
_____	_____
_____	_____
_____	_____
_____	_____

My Weekly "I WILL" Statements

I WILL: _____

I WILL: _____

I WILL: _____

I WILL: _____

I WILL: _____

My Next Step Strategy

For each category, each day write down one or more steps you will take to move you closer to what you envision.

Week of _____

	M	T	W	T	F	S	S
SPIRITUAL							
RELATIONSHIP							
HEALTH/FITNESS							
FINANCIAL							
BUSINESS/CAREER							
MINISTRY/SERVICE							
EDUCATION							
	WORD OF THE DAY:	WORD OF THE DAY:	WORD OF THE DAY:	WORD OF THE DAY:	WORD OF THE DAY:	WORD OF THE DAY:	WORD OF THE DAY:

Projects	Desired Outcomes	Deadline

To-Do List
Errands, emails, phone calls, etc.

☐ _____ ☐ _____
☐ _____ ☐ _____
☐ _____ ☐ _____
☐ _____ ☐ _____
☐ _____ ☐ _____
☐ _____ ☐ _____
☐ _____ ☐ _____
☐ _____ ☐ _____
☐ _____ ☐ _____
☐ _____ ☐ _____
☐ _____ ☐ _____
☐ _____ ☐ _____
☐ _____ ☐ _____
☐ _____ ☐ _____

Quick Note

Prayer Requests & Concerns

_____
_____
_____
_____
_____
_____
_____
_____
_____
_____
_____
_____
_____
_____
_____
_____
_____
_____
_____
_____

Daily Bible Reading Plan

MON _____

TUE _____

WED _____

THUR _____

FRI _____

SAT _____

SUN _____

Scriptures that speak to me

My Weekly "I AM" Statements

I AM: _____

I AM: _____

I AM: _____

I AM: _____

I AM: _____

Spiritual Downloads

Record what you saw or heard in the Spirit this week regarding God's vision for your life.

Divine Expectations	Praise Report
_____	_____

My Weekly "I WILL" Statements

I WILL: _____

I WILL: _____

I WILL: _____

I WILL: _____

I WILL: _____

My Next Step Strategy

For each category, each day write down one or more steps you will take to move you closer to what you envision.

	M	T	W	T	F	S	S
SPIRITUAL							
RELATIONSHIP							
HEALTH/FITNESS							
FINANCIAL							
BUSINESS/CAREER							
MINISTRY/SERVICE							
EDUCATION							
	WORD OF THE DAY:	WORD OF THE DAY:	WORD OF THE DAY:	WORD OF THE DAY:	WORD OF THE DAY:	WORD OF THE DAY:	WORD OF THE DAY:

Week of _____

Projects	Desired Outcomes	Deadline

To-Do List
Errands, emails, phone calls, etc.

☐ _____
☐ _____
☐ _____
☐ _____
☐ _____
☐ _____
☐ _____
☐ _____
☐ _____
☐ _____
☐ _____
☐ _____
☐ _____
☐ _____

☐ _____
☐ _____
☐ _____
☐ _____
☐ _____
☐ _____
☐ _____
☐ _____
☐ _____
☐ _____
☐ _____
☐ _____
☐ _____
☐ _____

Quick Note

Prayer Requests & Concerns

_____
_____
_____
_____
_____
_____
_____
_____
_____
_____
_____
_____
_____
_____
_____
_____
_____
_____
_____
_____
_____

Daily Bible Reading Plan

MON _____

TUE _____

WED _____

THUR _____

FRI _____

SAT _____

SUN _____

Scriptures that speak to me

My Weekly "I AM" Statements

I AM: _____

I AM: _____

I AM: _____

I AM: _____

I AM: _____

Spiritual Downloads

Record what you saw or heard in the Spirit this week regarding God's vision for your life.

Divine Expectations

_____
_____
_____
_____
_____
_____
_____

Praise Report

_____
_____
_____
_____
_____
_____
_____

My Weekly "I WILL" Statements

I WILL: _____

I WILL: _____

I WILL: _____

I WILL: _____

I WILL: _____

My Next Step Strategy

For each category, each day write down one or more steps you will take to move you closer to what you envision.

Week of _____

	M	T	W	T	F	S	S
SPIRITUAL							
RELATIONSHIP							
HEALTH/FITNESS							
FINANCIAL							
BUSINESS/CAREER							
MINISTRY/SERVICE							
EDUCATION							
	WORD OF THE DAY:	WORD OF THE DAY:	WORD OF THE DAY:	WORD OF THE DAY:	WORD OF THE DAY:	WORD OF THE DAY:	WORD OF THE DAY:

Projects	Desired Outcomes	Deadline

To-Do List
Errands, emails, phone calls, etc.

☐ _____
☐ _____
☐ _____
☐ _____
☐ _____
☐ _____
☐ _____
☐ _____
☐ _____
☐ _____
☐ _____
☐ _____
☐ _____
☐ _____
☐ _____

☐ _____
☐ _____
☐ _____
☐ _____
☐ _____
☐ _____
☐ _____
☐ _____
☐ _____
☐ _____
☐ _____
☐ _____
☐ _____
☐ _____
☐ _____

Quick Note

Prayer Requests & Concerns

_____
_____
_____
_____
_____
_____
_____
_____
_____
_____
_____
_____
_____
_____
_____
_____
_____
_____
_____
_____
_____

Daily Bible Reading Plan

MON _____

TUE _____

WED _____

THUR _____

FRI _____

SAT _____

SUN _____

Scriptures that speak to me

My Weekly "I AM" Statements

I AM: _____

I AM: _____

I AM: _____

I AM: _____

I AM: _____

Spiritual Downloads

Record what you saw or heard in the Spirit this week regarding God's vision for your life.

Divine Expectations	Praise Report
_____	_____
_____	_____
_____	_____
_____	_____
_____	_____
_____	_____
_____	_____

My Weekly "I WILL" Statements

I WILL: _____

I WILL: _____

I WILL: _____

I WILL: _____

I WILL: _____

My Next Step Strategy

For each category, each day write down one or more steps you will take to move you closer to what you envision.

Week of _____

	M	T	W	T	F	S	S
SPIRITUAL							
RELATIONSHIP							
HEALTH/FITNESS							
FINANCIAL							
BUSINESS/CAREER							
MINISTRY/SERVICE							
EDUCATION							
	WORD OF THE DAY:	WORD OF THE DAY:	WORD OF THE DAY:	WORD OF THE DAY:	WORD OF THE DAY:	WORD OF THE DAY:	WORD OF THE DAY:

120

Projects	Desired Outcomes	Deadline

To-Do List
Errands, emails, phone calls, etc.

- ☐ _____
- ☐ _____
- ☐ _____
- ☐ _____
- ☐ _____
- ☐ _____
- ☐ _____
- ☐ _____
- ☐ _____
- ☐ _____
- ☐ _____
- ☐ _____
- ☐ _____
- ☐ _____

- ☐ _____
- ☐ _____
- ☐ _____
- ☐ _____
- ☐ _____
- ☐ _____
- ☐ _____
- ☐ _____
- ☐ _____
- ☐ _____
- ☐ _____
- ☐ _____
- ☐ _____
- ☐ _____

Quick Note

Prayer Requests & Concerns

_____
_____
_____
_____
_____
_____
_____
_____
_____
_____
_____
_____
_____
_____
_____
_____
_____
_____
_____
_____
_____
_____

Daily Bible Reading Plan

MON _____

TUE _____

WED _____

THUR _____

FRI _____

SAT _____

SUN _____

Scriptures that speak to me

My Weekly "I AM" Statements

I AM: _____

I AM: _____

I AM: _____

I AM: _____

I AM: _____

Spiritual Downloads

Record what you saw or heard in the Spirit this week regarding God's vision for your life.

Divine Expectations	Praise Report
_____	_____
_____	_____
_____	_____
_____	_____
_____	_____
_____	_____
_____	_____

My Weekly "I WILL" Statements

I WILL: _____

I WILL: _____

I WILL: _____

I WILL: _____

I WILL: _____

My Next Step Strategy

For each category, each day write down one or more steps you will take to move you closer to what you envision.

Week of _____

	M	T	W	T	F	S	S
SPIRITUAL							
RELATIONSHIP							
HEALTH/FITNESS							
FINANCIAL							
BUSINESS/CAREER							
MINISTRY/SERVICE							
EDUCATION							
	WORD OF THE DAY:	WORD OF THE DAY:	WORD OF THE DAY:	WORD OF THE DAY:	WORD OF THE DAY:	WORD OF THE DAY:	WORD OF THE DAY:

Projects	Desired Outcomes	Deadline

To-Do List
Errands, emails, phone calls, etc.

☐ _____
☐ _____
☐ _____
☐ _____
☐ _____
☐ _____
☐ _____
☐ _____
☐ _____
☐ _____
☐ _____
☐ _____
☐ _____
☐ _____
☐ _____

☐ _____
☐ _____
☐ _____
☐ _____
☐ _____
☐ _____
☐ _____
☐ _____
☐ _____
☐ _____
☐ _____
☐ _____
☐ _____
☐ _____
☐ _____

Quick Note

Prayer Requests & Concerns

_____
_____
_____
_____
_____
_____
_____
_____
_____
_____
_____
_____
_____
_____
_____
_____
_____
_____
_____
_____
_____
_____

Daily Bible Reading Plan

MON _____

TUE _____

WED _____

THUR _____

FRI _____

SAT _____

SUN _____

Scriptures that speak to me

My Weekly "I AM" Statements

I AM: _____

I AM: _____

I AM: _____

I AM: _____

I AM: _____

Spiritual Downloads

Record what you saw or heard in the Spirit this week regarding God's vision for your life.

Divine Expectations

_____
_____
_____
_____
_____
_____
_____

Praise Report

_____
_____
_____
_____
_____
_____
_____

My Weekly "I WILL" Statements

I WILL: _____

I WILL: _____

I WILL: _____

I WILL: _____

I WILL: _____

My Next Step Strategy

For each category, each day write down one or more steps you will take to move you closer to what you envision.

Week of _____

	M	T	W	T	F	S	S
SPIRITUAL							
RELATIONSHIP							
HEALTH/FITNESS							
FINANCIAL							
BUSINESS/CAREER							
MINISTRY/SERVICE							
EDUCATION							
	WORD OF THE DAY:	WORD OF THE DAY:	WORD OF THE DAY:	WORD OF THE DAY:	WORD OF THE DAY:	WORD OF THE DAY:	WORD OF THE DAY:

Projects	Desired Outcomes	Deadline

To-Do List
Errands, emails, phone calls, etc.

- ☐ _____
- ☐ _____
- ☐ _____
- ☐ _____
- ☐ _____
- ☐ _____
- ☐ _____
- ☐ _____
- ☐ _____
- ☐ _____
- ☐ _____
- ☐ _____
- ☐ _____
- ☐ _____

- ☐ _____
- ☐ _____
- ☐ _____
- ☐ _____
- ☐ _____
- ☐ _____
- ☐ _____
- ☐ _____
- ☐ _____
- ☐ _____
- ☐ _____
- ☐ _____
- ☐ _____
- ☐ _____

Quick Note

Prayer Requests & Concerns

_____
_____
_____
_____
_____
_____
_____
_____
_____
_____
_____
_____
_____
_____
_____
_____
_____
_____
_____
_____
_____
_____

Daily Bible Reading Plan

MON _____

TUE _____

WED _____

THUR _____

FRI _____

SAT _____

SUN _____

Scriptures that speak to me

My Weekly "I AM" Statements

I AM: _____

I AM: _____

I AM: _____

I AM: _____

I AM: _____

Spiritual Downloads

Record what you saw or heard in the Spirit this week regarding God's vision for your life.

Divine Expectations	Praise Report
_____	_____
_____	_____
_____	_____
_____	_____
_____	_____
_____	_____
_____	_____

My Weekly "I WILL" Statements

I WILL: _____

I WILL: _____

I WILL: _____

I WILL: _____

I WILL: _____

My Next Step Strategy

For each category, each day write down one or more steps you will take to move you closer to what you envision.

Week of _____

	M	T	W	T	F	S	S
SPIRITUAL							
RELATIONSHIP							
HEALTH/FITNESS							
FINANCIAL							
BUSINESS/CAREER							
MINISTRY/SERVICE							
EDUCATION							
	WORD OF THE DAY:	WORD OF THE DAY:	WORD OF THE DAY:	WORD OF THE DAY:	WORD OF THE DAY:	WORD OF THE DAY:	WORD OF THE DAY:

Projects	Desired Outcomes	Deadline

To-Do List
Errands, emails, phone calls, etc.

- ☐ _____
- ☐ _____
- ☐ _____
- ☐ _____
- ☐ _____
- ☐ _____
- ☐ _____
- ☐ _____
- ☐ _____
- ☐ _____
- ☐ _____
- ☐ _____
- ☐ _____
- ☐ _____
- ☐ _____

- ☐ _____
- ☐ _____
- ☐ _____
- ☐ _____
- ☐ _____
- ☐ _____
- ☐ _____
- ☐ _____
- ☐ _____
- ☐ _____
- ☐ _____
- ☐ _____
- ☐ _____
- ☐ _____
- ☐ _____

Quick Note

Prayer Requests & Concerns

_____
_____
_____
_____
_____
_____
_____
_____
_____
_____
_____
_____
_____
_____
_____
_____
_____
_____
_____
_____
_____

Daily Bible Reading Plan

MON _____

TUE _____

WED _____

THUR _____

FRI _____

SAT _____

SUN _____

Scriptures that speak to me

My Weekly "I AM" Statements

I AM: _____

I AM: _____

I AM: _____

I AM: _____

I AM: _____

Spiritual Downloads

Record what you saw or heard in the Spirit this week regarding God's vision for your life.

Divine Expectations

_____
_____
_____
_____
_____
_____
_____

Praise Report

_____
_____
_____
_____
_____
_____
_____

My Weekly "I WILL" Statements

I WILL: _____

I WILL: _____

I WILL: _____

I WILL: _____

I WILL: _____

My Next Step Strategy

For each category, each day write down one or more steps you will take to move you closer to what you envision.

	M	T	W	T	F	S	S
SPIRITUAL							
RELATIONSHIP							
HEALTH/FITNESS							
FINANCIAL							
BUSINESS/CAREER							
MINISTRY/SERVICE							
EDUCATION							
	WORD OF THE DAY:	WORD OF THE DAY:	WORD OF THE DAY:	WORD OF THE DAY:	WORD OF THE DAY:	WORD OF THE DAY:	WORD OF THE DAY:

Week of _____

Projects	Desired Outcomes	Deadline

To-Do List
Errands, emails, phone calls, etc.

- ☐ _____
- ☐ _____
- ☐ _____
- ☐ _____
- ☐ _____
- ☐ _____
- ☐ _____
- ☐ _____
- ☐ _____
- ☐ _____
- ☐ _____
- ☐ _____
- ☐ _____
- ☐ _____

- ☐ _____
- ☐ _____
- ☐ _____
- ☐ _____
- ☐ _____
- ☐ _____
- ☐ _____
- ☐ _____
- ☐ _____
- ☐ _____
- ☐ _____
- ☐ _____
- ☐ _____
- ☐ _____

Quick Note

Prayer Requests & Concerns

_____
_____
_____
_____
_____
_____
_____
_____
_____
_____
_____
_____
_____
_____
_____
_____
_____
_____
_____
_____
_____
_____

Daily Bible Reading Plan

MON _____

TUE _____

WED _____

THUR _____

FRI _____

SAT _____

SUN _____

Scriptures that speak to me

My Weekly "I AM" Statements

I AM: _____

I AM: _____

I AM: _____

I AM: _____

I AM: _____

Spiritual Downloads

Record what you saw or heard in the Spirit this week regarding God's vision for your life.

Divine Expectations

_____
_____
_____
_____
_____
_____
_____

Praise Report

_____
_____
_____
_____
_____
_____
_____

My Weekly "I WILL" Statements

I WILL: _____

I WILL: _____

I WILL: _____

I WILL: _____

I WILL: _____

My Next Step Strategy

For each category, each day write down one or more steps you will take to move you closer to what you envision.

Week of _____

	M	T	W	T	F	S	S
SPIRITUAL							
RELATIONSHIP							
HEALTH/FITNESS							
FINANCIAL							
BUSINESS/CAREER							
MINISTRY/SERVICE							
EDUCATION							
	WORD OF THE DAY:	WORD OF THE DAY:	WORD OF THE DAY:	WORD OF THE DAY:	WORD OF THE DAY:	WORD OF THE DAY:	WORD OF THE DAY:

Projects	Desired Outcomes	Deadline

To-Do List
Errands, emails, phone calls, etc.

☐ _____
☐ _____
☐ _____
☐ _____
☐ _____
☐ _____
☐ _____
☐ _____
☐ _____
☐ _____
☐ _____
☐ _____
☐ _____
☐ _____
☐ _____

☐ _____
☐ _____
☐ _____
☐ _____
☐ _____
☐ _____
☐ _____
☐ _____
☐ _____
☐ _____
☐ _____
☐ _____
☐ _____
☐ _____
☐ _____

Quick Note

Prayer Requests & Concerns

_____
_____
_____
_____
_____
_____
_____
_____
_____
_____
_____
_____
_____
_____
_____
_____
_____
_____
_____
_____

Daily Bible Reading Plan

MON _____

TUE _____

WED _____

THUR _____

FRI _____

SAT _____

SUN _____

Scriptures that speak to me

My Weekly "I AM" Statements

I AM: _____

I AM: _____

I AM: _____

I AM: _____

I AM: _____

Spiritual Downloads

Record what you saw or heard in the Spirit this week regarding God's vision for your life.

Divine Expectations	Praise Report
_____	_____
_____	_____
_____	_____
_____	_____
_____	_____
_____	_____
_____	

My Weekly "I WILL" Statements

I WILL: _____

I WILL: _____

I WILL: _____

I WILL: _____

I WILL: _____

My Next Step Strategy

For each category, each day write down one or more steps you will take to move you closer to what you envision.

	M	T	W	T	F	S	S
SPIRITUAL							
RELATIONSHIP							
HEALTH/FITNESS							
FINANCIAL							
BUSINESS/CAREER							
MINISTRY/SERVICE							
EDUCATION	WORD OF THE DAY:	WORD OF THE DAY:	WORD OF THE DAY:	WORD OF THE DAY:	WORD OF THE DAY:	WORD OF THE DAY:	WORD OF THE DAY:

Week of _____

Projects	Desired Outcomes	Deadline

To-Do List
Errands, emails, phone calls, etc.

☐ _____
☐ _____
☐ _____
☐ _____
☐ _____
☐ _____
☐ _____
☐ _____
☐ _____
☐ _____
☐ _____
☐ _____
☐ _____
☐ _____
☐ _____

☐ _____
☐ _____
☐ _____
☐ _____
☐ _____
☐ _____
☐ _____
☐ _____
☐ _____
☐ _____
☐ _____
☐ _____
☐ _____
☐ _____
☐ _____

Quick Note

Prayer Requests & Concerns

_____
_____
_____
_____
_____
_____
_____
_____
_____
_____
_____
_____
_____
_____
_____
_____
_____
_____
_____
_____
_____
_____

Daily Bible Reading Plan

MON _____

TUE _____

WED _____

THUR _____

FRI _____

SAT _____

SUN _____

Scriptures that speak to me

My Weekly "I AM" Statements

I AM: _____

I AM: _____

I AM: _____

I AM: _____

I AM: _____

Spiritual Downloads

Record what you saw or heard in the Spirit this week regarding God's vision for your life.

Divine Expectations	Praise Report
_____	_____
_____	_____
_____	_____
_____	_____
_____	_____
_____	_____
_____	_____

My Weekly "I WILL" Statements

I WILL: _____

I WILL: _____

I WILL: _____

I WILL: _____

I WILL: _____

My Next Step Strategy

For each category, each day write down one or more steps you will take to move you closer to what you envision.

	M	T	W	T	F	S	S
SPIRITUAL							
RELATIONSHIP							
HEALTH/FITNESS							
FINANCIAL							
BUSINESS/CAREER							
MINISTRY/SERVICE							
EDUCATION							
	WORD OF THE DAY:	WORD OF THE DAY:	WORD OF THE DAY:	WORD OF THE DAY:	WORD OF THE DAY:	WORD OF THE DAY:	WORD OF THE DAY:

Week of ____

Projects	Desired Outcomes	Deadline

To-Do List
Errands, emails, phone calls, etc.

- ☐ _____
- ☐ _____
- ☐ _____
- ☐ _____
- ☐ _____
- ☐ _____
- ☐ _____
- ☐ _____
- ☐ _____
- ☐ _____
- ☐ _____
- ☐ _____
- ☐ _____
- ☐ _____
- ☐ _____

- ☐ _____
- ☐ _____
- ☐ _____
- ☐ _____
- ☐ _____
- ☐ _____
- ☐ _____
- ☐ _____
- ☐ _____
- ☐ _____
- ☐ _____
- ☐ _____
- ☐ _____
- ☐ _____
- ☐ _____

Quick Note

Prayer Requests & Concerns

_____
_____
_____
_____
_____
_____
_____
_____
_____
_____
_____
_____
_____
_____
_____
_____
_____
_____
_____
_____

Daily Bible Reading Plan

MON _____

TUE _____

WED _____

THUR _____

FRI _____

SAT _____

SUN _____

Scriptures that speak to me

My Weekly "I AM" Statements

I AM: _____

I AM: _____

I AM: _____

I AM: _____

I AM: _____

Spiritual Downloads

Record what you saw or heard in the Spirit this week regarding God's vision for your life.

Divine Expectations	Praise Report
_____	_____
_____	_____
_____	_____
_____	_____
_____	_____
_____	_____
_____	_____

My Weekly "I WILL" Statements

I WILL: _____

I WILL: _____

I WILL: _____

I WILL: _____

I WILL: _____

My Next Step Strategy

For each category, each day write down one or more steps you will take to move you closer to what you envision.

Week of _____

	M	T	W	T	F	S	S
SPIRITUAL							
RELATIONSHIP							
HEALTH/FITNESS							
FINANCIAL							
BUSINESS/CAREER							
MINISTRY/SERVICE							
EDUCATION							
	WORD OF THE DAY:	WORD OF THE DAY:	WORD OF THE DAY:	WORD OF THE DAY:	WORD OF THE DAY:	WORD OF THE DAY:	WORD OF THE DAY:

Projects	Desired Outcomes	Deadline

To-Do List
Errands, emails, phone calls, etc.

- ☐ _____
- ☐ _____
- ☐ _____
- ☐ _____
- ☐ _____
- ☐ _____
- ☐ _____
- ☐ _____
- ☐ _____
- ☐ _____
- ☐ _____
- ☐ _____
- ☐ _____
- ☐ _____

- ☐ _____
- ☐ _____
- ☐ _____
- ☐ _____
- ☐ _____
- ☐ _____
- ☐ _____
- ☐ _____
- ☐ _____
- ☐ _____
- ☐ _____
- ☐ _____
- ☐ _____
- ☐ _____

Quick Note

Prayer Requests & Concerns

_____
_____
_____
_____
_____
_____
_____
_____
_____
_____
_____
_____
_____
_____
_____
_____
_____
_____
_____
_____

Daily Bible Reading Plan

MON _____

TUE _____

WED _____

THUR _____

FRI _____

SAT _____

SUN _____

Scriptures that speak to me

My Weekly "I AM" Statements

I AM: _____

I AM: _____

I AM: _____

I AM: _____

I AM: _____

Spiritual Downloads

Record what you saw or heard in the Spirit this week regarding God's vision for your life.

Divine Expectations	Praise Report
_____	_____
_____	_____
_____	_____
_____	_____
_____	_____
_____	_____
_____	_____

My Weekly "I WILL" Statements

I WILL: _____

I WILL: _____

I WILL: _____

I WILL: _____

I WILL: _____

My Next Step Strategy

For each category, each day write down one or more steps you will take to move you closer to what you envision.

	M	T	W	T	F	S	S
SPIRITUAL							
RELATIONSHIP							
HEALTH/FITNESS							
FINANCIAL							
BUSINESS/CAREER							
MINISTRY/SERVICE							
EDUCATION							
	WORD OF THE DAY:	WORD OF THE DAY:	WORD OF THE DAY:	WORD OF THE DAY:	WORD OF THE DAY:	WORD OF THE DAY:	WORD OF THE DAY:

Week of _____

Projects	Desired Outcomes	Deadline

To-Do List
Errands, emails, phone calls, etc.

- ☐ _____
- ☐ _____
- ☐ _____
- ☐ _____
- ☐ _____
- ☐ _____
- ☐ _____
- ☐ _____
- ☐ _____
- ☐ _____
- ☐ _____
- ☐ _____
- ☐ _____
- ☐ _____
- ☐ _____

- ☐ _____
- ☐ _____
- ☐ _____
- ☐ _____
- ☐ _____
- ☐ _____
- ☐ _____
- ☐ _____
- ☐ _____
- ☐ _____
- ☐ _____
- ☐ _____
- ☐ _____
- ☐ _____

Quick Note

Prayer Requests & Concerns

_____
_____
_____
_____
_____
_____
_____
_____
_____
_____
_____
_____
_____
_____
_____
_____
_____
_____
_____
_____

Daily Bible Reading Plan

MON _____

TUE _____

WED _____

THUR _____

FRI _____

SAT _____

SUN _____

Scriptures that speak to me

My Weekly "I AM" Statements

I AM: _____

I AM: _____

I AM: _____

I AM: _____

I AM: _____

Spiritual Downloads

Record what you saw or heard in the Spirit this week regarding God's vision for your life.

Divine Expectations	Praise Report
_____	_____
_____	_____
_____	_____
_____	_____
_____	_____
_____	_____
_____	_____

My Weekly "I WILL" Statements

I WILL: _____

I WILL: _____

I WILL: _____

I WILL: _____

I WILL: _____

My Next Step Strategy
For each category, each day write down one or more steps you will take to move you closer to what you envision.

Week of _____

	M	T	W	T	F	S	S
SPIRITUAL							
RELATIONSHIP							
HEALTH/FITNESS							
FINANCIAL							
BUSINESS/CAREER							
MINISTRY/SERVICE							
EDUCATION							
	WORD OF THE DAY:	WORD OF THE DAY:	WORD OF THE DAY:	WORD OF THE DAY:	WORD OF THE DAY:	WORD OF THE DAY:	WORD OF THE DAY:

Projects	Desired Outcomes	Deadline

To-Do List
Errands, emails, phone calls, etc.

☐ _____
☐ _____
☐ _____
☐ _____
☐ _____
☐ _____
☐ _____
☐ _____
☐ _____
☐ _____
☐ _____
☐ _____
☐ _____
☐ _____
☐ _____

☐ _____
☐ _____
☐ _____
☐ _____
☐ _____
☐ _____
☐ _____
☐ _____
☐ _____
☐ _____
☐ _____
☐ _____
☐ _____
☐ _____
☐ _____

Quick Note

Prayer Requests & Concerns

_____
_____
_____
_____
_____
_____
_____
_____
_____
_____
_____
_____
_____
_____
_____
_____
_____
_____
_____
_____
_____

Daily Bible Reading Plan

MON _____

TUE _____

WED _____

THUR _____

FRI _____

SAT _____

SUN _____

Scriptures that speak to me

My Weekly "I AM" Statements

I AM: _____

I AM: _____

I AM: _____

I AM: _____

I AM: _____

Spiritual Downloads

Record what you saw or heard in the Spirit this week regarding God's vision for your life.

Divine Expectations	Praise Report
_____	_____
_____	_____
_____	_____
_____	_____
_____	_____
_____	_____

My Weekly "I WILL" Statements

I WILL: _____

I WILL: _____

I WILL: _____

I WILL: _____

I WILL: _____

My Next Step Strategy

For each category, each day write down one or more steps you will take to move you closer to what you envision.

Week of _____

	M	T	W	T	F	S	S
SPIRITUAL							
RELATIONSHIP							
HEALTH/FITNESS							
FINANCIAL							
BUSINESS/CAREER							
MINISTRY/SERVICE							
EDUCATION							
	WORD OF THE DAY:	WORD OF THE DAY:	WORD OF THE DAY:	WORD OF THE DAY:	WORD OF THE DAY:	WORD OF THE DAY:	WORD OF THE DAY:

Projects	Desired Outcomes	Deadline

To-Do List
Errands, emails, phone calls, etc.

☐ _____ ☐ _____
☐ _____ ☐ _____
☐ _____ ☐ _____
☐ _____ ☐ _____
☐ _____ ☐ _____
☐ _____ ☐ _____
☐ _____ ☐ _____
☐ _____ ☐ _____
☐ _____ ☐ _____
☐ _____ ☐ _____
☐ _____ ☐ _____
☐ _____ ☐ _____
☐ _____ ☐ _____
☐ _____ ☐ _____
☐ _____ ☐ _____

Quick Note

Prayer Requests & Concerns

_____
_____
_____
_____
_____
_____
_____
_____
_____
_____
_____
_____
_____
_____
_____
_____
_____
_____
_____
_____
_____

Daily Bible Reading Plan

MON _____

TUE _____

WED _____

THUR _____

FRI _____

SAT _____

SUN _____

Scriptures that speak to me

My Weekly "I AM" Statements

I AM: _____

I AM: _____

I AM: _____

I AM: _____

I AM: _____

Spiritual Downloads

Record what you saw or heard in the Spirit this week regarding God's vision for your life.

Divine Expectations	Praise Report
_____	_____
_____	_____
_____	_____
_____	_____
_____	_____
_____	_____
_____	

My Weekly "I WILL" Statements

I WILL: _____

I WILL: _____

I WILL: _____

I WILL: _____

I WILL: _____

My Next Step Strategy

For each category, each day write down one or more steps you will take to move you closer to what you envision.

Week of _____

	M	T	W	T	F	S	S
SPIRITUAL							
RELATIONSHIP							
HEALTH/FITNESS							
FINANCIAL							
BUSINESS/CAREER							
MINISTRY/SERVICE							
EDUCATION							
	WORD OF THE DAY:	WORD OF THE DAY:	WORD OF THE DAY:	WORD OF THE DAY:	WORD OF THE DAY:	WORD OF THE DAY:	WORD OF THE DAY:

Projects	Desired Outcomes	Deadline

To-Do List
Errands, emails, phone calls, etc.

☐ _____
☐ _____
☐ _____
☐ _____
☐ _____
☐ _____
☐ _____
☐ _____
☐ _____
☐ _____
☐ _____
☐ _____
☐ _____
☐ _____
☐ _____

☐ _____
☐ _____
☐ _____
☐ _____
☐ _____
☐ _____
☐ _____
☐ _____
☐ _____
☐ _____
☐ _____
☐ _____
☐ _____
☐ _____
☐ _____

Quick Note

Prayer Requests & Concerns

_____
_____
_____
_____
_____
_____
_____
_____
_____
_____
_____
_____
_____
_____
_____
_____
_____
_____
_____
_____

Daily Bible Reading Plan

MON _____

TUE _____

WED _____

THUR _____

FRI _____

SAT _____

SUN _____

Scriptures that speak to me

My Weekly "I AM" Statements

I AM: _____

I AM: _____

I AM: _____

I AM: _____

I AM: _____

Spiritual Downloads

Record what you saw or heard in the Spirit this week regarding God's vision for your life.

Divine Expectations	Praise Report
_____	_____
_____	_____
_____	_____
_____	_____
_____	_____
_____	_____
_____	_____

My Weekly "I WILL" Statements

I WILL: _____

I WILL: _____

I WILL: _____

I WILL: _____

I WILL: _____

My Next Step Strategy

For each category, each day write down one or more steps you will take to move you closer to what you envision.

Week of _____	M	T	W	T	F	S	S
SPIRITUAL							
RELATIONSHIP							
HEALTH/FITNESS							
FINANCIAL							
BUSINESS/CAREER							
MINISTRY/SERVICE							
EDUCATION							
	WORD OF THE DAY:	WORD OF THE DAY:	WORD OF THE DAY:	WORD OF THE DAY:	WORD OF THE DAY:	WORD OF THE DAY:	WORD OF THE DAY:

Projects	Desired Outcomes	Deadline

To-Do List
Errands, emails, phone calls, etc.

☐ _____
☐ _____
☐ _____
☐ _____
☐ _____
☐ _____
☐ _____
☐ _____
☐ _____
☐ _____
☐ _____
☐ _____
☐ _____
☐ _____
☐ _____

☐ _____
☐ _____
☐ _____
☐ _____
☐ _____
☐ _____
☐ _____
☐ _____
☐ _____
☐ _____
☐ _____
☐ _____
☐ _____
☐ _____

Quick Note

Prayer Requests & Concerns

_____
_____
_____
_____
_____
_____
_____
_____
_____
_____
_____
_____
_____
_____
_____
_____
_____
_____
_____
_____
_____

Daily Bible Reading Plan

MON _____

TUE _____

WED _____

THUR _____

FRI _____

SAT _____

SUN _____

Scriptures that speak to me

My Weekly "I AM" Statements

I AM: _____

I AM: _____

I AM: _____

I AM: _____

I AM: _____

Spiritual Downloads

Record what you saw or heard in the Spirit this week regarding God's vision for your life.

Divine Expectations

_____
_____
_____
_____
_____
_____
_____

Praise Report

_____
_____
_____
_____
_____
_____
_____

My Weekly "I WILL" Statements

I WILL: _____

I WILL: _____

I WILL: _____

I WILL: _____

I WILL: _____

My Next Step Strategy

For each category, each day write down one or more steps you will take to move you closer to what you envision.

Week of _____

	M	T	W	T	F	S	S
SPIRITUAL							
RELATIONSHIP							
HEALTH/FITNESS							
FINANCIAL							
BUSINESS/CAREER							
MINISTRY/SERVICE							
EDUCATION							
	WORD OF THE DAY:	WORD OF THE DAY:	WORD OF THE DAY:	WORD OF THE DAY:	WORD OF THE DAY:	WORD OF THE DAY:	WORD OF THE DAY:

Projects	Desired Outcomes	Deadline

To-Do List
Errands, emails, phone calls, etc.

- ☐ _____
- ☐ _____
- ☐ _____
- ☐ _____
- ☐ _____
- ☐ _____
- ☐ _____
- ☐ _____
- ☐ _____
- ☐ _____
- ☐ _____
- ☐ _____
- ☐ _____
- ☐ _____
- ☐ _____

- ☐ _____
- ☐ _____
- ☐ _____
- ☐ _____
- ☐ _____
- ☐ _____
- ☐ _____
- ☐ _____
- ☐ _____
- ☐ _____
- ☐ _____
- ☐ _____
- ☐ _____
- ☐ _____
- ☐ _____

Quick Note

Prayer Requests & Concerns

_____
_____
_____
_____
_____
_____
_____
_____
_____
_____
_____
_____
_____
_____
_____
_____
_____
_____
_____
_____
_____

Daily Bible Reading Plan

MON _____

TUE _____

WED _____

THUR _____

FRI _____

SAT _____

SUN _____

Scriptures that speak to me

My Weekly "I AM" Statements

I AM: _____

I AM: _____

I AM: _____

I AM: _____

I AM: _____

Spiritual Downloads

Record what you saw or heard in the Spirit this week regarding God's vision for your life.

Divine Expectations	Praise Report
_____	_____
_____	_____
_____	_____
_____	_____
_____	_____
_____	_____
_____	_____

My Weekly "I WILL" Statements

I WILL: _____

I WILL: _____

I WILL: _____

I WILL: _____

I WILL: _____

My Next Step Strategy

For each category, each day write down one or more steps you will take to move you closer to what you envision.

Week of _____

	M	T	W	T	F	S	S
SPIRITUAL							
RELATIONSHIP							
HEALTH/FITNESS							
FINANCIAL							
BUSINESS/CAREER							
MINISTRY/SERVICE							
EDUCATION							
	WORD OF THE DAY:	WORD OF THE DAY:	WORD OF THE DAY:	WORD OF THE DAY:	WORD OF THE DAY:	WORD OF THE DAY:	WORD OF THE DAY:

Projects	Desired Outcomes	Deadline

To-Do List
Errands, emails, phone calls, etc.

☐ _____
☐ _____
☐ _____
☐ _____
☐ _____
☐ _____
☐ _____
☐ _____
☐ _____
☐ _____
☐ _____
☐ _____
☐ _____
☐ _____
☐ _____

☐ _____
☐ _____
☐ _____
☐ _____
☐ _____
☐ _____
☐ _____
☐ _____
☐ _____
☐ _____
☐ _____
☐ _____
☐ _____
☐ _____
☐ _____

Quick Note

Prayer Requests & Concerns

_____
_____
_____
_____
_____
_____
_____
_____
_____
_____
_____
_____
_____
_____
_____
_____
_____
_____
_____
_____

Daily Bible Reading Plan

MON _____

TUE _____

WED _____

THUR _____

FRI _____

SAT _____

SUN _____

Scriptures that speak to me

My Weekly "I AM" Statements

I AM: _____

I AM: _____

I AM: _____

I AM: _____

I AM: _____

Spiritual Downloads

Record what you saw or heard in the Spirit this week regarding God's vision for your life.

Divine Expectations	Praise Report
_____	_____
_____	_____
_____	_____
_____	_____
_____	_____
_____	_____
_____	_____

My Weekly "I WILL" Statements

I WILL: _____

I WILL: _____

I WILL: _____

I WILL: _____

I WILL: _____

My Next Step Strategy

For each category, each day write down one or more steps you will take to move you closer to what you envision.

Week of _____

	M	T	W	T	F	S	S
SPIRITUAL							
RELATIONSHIP							
HEALTH/FITNESS							
FINANCIAL							
BUSINESS/CAREER							
MINISTRY/SERVICE							
EDUCATION							
	WORD OF THE DAY:	WORD OF THE DAY:	WORD OF THE DAY:	WORD OF THE DAY:	WORD OF THE DAY:	WORD OF THE DAY:	WORD OF THE DAY:

Projects	Desired Outcomes	Deadline

To-Do List
Errands, emails, phone calls, etc.

☐ _____
☐ _____
☐ _____
☐ _____
☐ _____
☐ _____
☐ _____
☐ _____
☐ _____
☐ _____
☐ _____
☐ _____
☐ _____
☐ _____

☐ _____
☐ _____
☐ _____
☐ _____
☐ _____
☐ _____
☐ _____
☐ _____
☐ _____
☐ _____
☐ _____
☐ _____
☐ _____
☐ _____

Quick Note

Prayer Requests & Concerns

_____
_____
_____
_____
_____
_____
_____
_____
_____
_____
_____
_____
_____
_____
_____
_____
_____
_____
_____
_____

Daily Bible Reading Plan

MON _____

TUE _____

WED _____

THUR _____

FRI _____

SAT _____

SUN _____

Scriptures that speak to me

My Weekly "I AM" Statements

I AM: _____

I AM: _____

I AM: _____

I AM: _____

I AM: _____

Spiritual Downloads

Record what you saw or heard in the Spirit this week regarding God's vision for your life.

Divine Expectations	Praise Report
_____	_____
_____	_____
_____	_____
_____	_____
_____	_____
_____	_____
_____	

My Weekly "I WILL" Statements

I WILL: _____

I WILL: _____

I WILL: _____

I WILL: _____

I WILL: _____

My Next Step Strategy

For each category, each day write down one or more steps you will take to move you closer to what you envision.

	M	T	W	T	F	S	S
SPIRITUAL							
RELATIONSHIP							
HEALTH/FITNESS							
FINANCIAL							
BUSINESS/CAREER							
MINISTRY/SERVICE							
EDUCATION							
	WORD OF THE DAY:	WORD OF THE DAY:	WORD OF THE DAY:	WORD OF THE DAY:	WORD OF THE DAY:	WORD OF THE DAY:	WORD OF THE DAY:

Week of _____

Projects	Desired Outcomes	Deadline

To-Do List
Errands, emails, phone calls, etc.

☐ _____
☐ _____
☐ _____
☐ _____
☐ _____
☐ _____
☐ _____
☐ _____
☐ _____
☐ _____
☐ _____
☐ _____
☐ _____
☐ _____
☐ _____

☐ _____
☐ _____
☐ _____
☐ _____
☐ _____
☐ _____
☐ _____
☐ _____
☐ _____
☐ _____
☐ _____
☐ _____
☐ _____
☐ _____
☐ _____

Quick Note

Prayer Requests & Concerns

_____
_____
_____
_____
_____
_____
_____
_____
_____
_____
_____
_____
_____
_____
_____
_____
_____
_____
_____
_____
_____
_____

Daily Bible Reading Plan

MON _____

TUE _____

WED _____

THUR _____

FRI _____

SAT _____

SUN _____

Scriptures that speak to me

My Weekly "I AM" Statements

I AM: _____

I AM: _____

I AM: _____

I AM: _____

I AM: _____

Spiritual Downloads

Record what you saw or heard in the Spirit this week regarding God's vision for your life.

Divine Expectations	Praise Report
_____	_____
_____	_____
_____	_____
_____	_____
_____	_____
_____	_____
_____	

My Weekly "I WILL" Statements

I WILL: _____

I WILL: _____

I WILL: _____

I WILL: _____

I WILL: _____

My Next Step Strategy

For each category, each day write down one or more steps you will take to move you closer to what you envision.

	M	T	W	T	F	S	S
SPIRITUAL							
RELATIONSHIP							
HEALTH/FITNESS							
FINANCIAL							
BUSINESS/CAREER							
MINISTRY/SERVICE							
EDUCATION							
	WORD OF THE DAY:	WORD OF THE DAY:	WORD OF THE DAY:	WORD OF THE DAY:	WORD OF THE DAY:	WORD OF THE DAY:	WORD OF THE DAY:

Week of _____

Projects	Desired Outcomes	Deadline

To-Do List
Errands, emails, phone calls, etc.

☐ _____
☐ _____
☐ _____
☐ _____
☐ _____
☐ _____
☐ _____
☐ _____
☐ _____
☐ _____
☐ _____
☐ _____
☐ _____
☐ _____
☐ _____

☐ _____
☐ _____
☐ _____
☐ _____
☐ _____
☐ _____
☐ _____
☐ _____
☐ _____
☐ _____
☐ _____
☐ _____
☐ _____
☐ _____
☐ _____

Quick Note

Prayer Requests & Concerns

_____
_____
_____
_____
_____
_____
_____
_____
_____
_____
_____
_____
_____
_____
_____
_____
_____
_____
_____
_____

Daily Bible Reading Plan

MON _____

TUE _____

WED _____

THUR _____

FRI _____

SAT _____

SUN _____

Scriptures that speak to me

My Weekly "I AM" Statements

I AM: _____

I AM: _____

I AM: _____

I AM: _____

I AM: _____

Spiritual Downloads

Record what you saw or heard in the Spirit this week regarding God's vision for your life.

Divine Expectations

_____

_____

_____

_____

_____

_____

_____

Praise Report

_____

_____

_____

_____

_____

_____

_____

My Weekly "I WILL" Statements

I WILL: _____

I WILL: _____

I WILL: _____

I WILL: _____

I WILL: _____

My Next Step Strategy

For each category, each day write down one or more steps you will take to move you closer to what you envision.

Week of _____

	M	T	W	T	F	S	S
SPIRITUAL							
RELATIONSHIP							
HEALTH/FITNESS							
FINANCIAL							
BUSINESS/CAREER							
MINISTRY/SERVICE							
EDUCATION							
	WORD OF THE DAY:	WORD OF THE DAY:	WORD OF THE DAY:	WORD OF THE DAY:	WORD OF THE DAY:	WORD OF THE DAY:	WORD OF THE DAY:

Projects	Desired Outcomes	Deadline

To-Do List
Errands, emails, phone calls, etc.

☐ _____
☐ _____
☐ _____
☐ _____
☐ _____
☐ _____
☐ _____
☐ _____
☐ _____
☐ _____
☐ _____
☐ _____
☐ _____
☐ _____

☐ _____
☐ _____
☐ _____
☐ _____
☐ _____
☐ _____
☐ _____
☐ _____
☐ _____
☐ _____
☐ _____
☐ _____
☐ _____
☐ _____

Quick Note

Prayer Requests & Concerns

_____
_____
_____
_____
_____
_____
_____
_____
_____
_____
_____
_____
_____
_____
_____
_____
_____
_____
_____
_____
_____

Daily Bible Reading Plan

MON _____

TUE _____

WED _____

THUR _____

FRI _____

SAT _____

SUN _____

Scriptures that speak to me

My Weekly "I AM" Statements

I AM: _____

I AM: _____

I AM: _____

I AM: _____

I AM: _____

Spiritual Downloads

Record what you saw or heard in the Spirit this week regarding God's vision for your life.

Divine Expectations	Praise Report
_____	_____
_____	_____
_____	_____
_____	_____
_____	_____
_____	_____
_____	

My Weekly "I WILL" Statements

I WILL: _____

I WILL: _____

I WILL: _____

I WILL: _____

I WILL: _____

My Next Step Strategy

For each category, each day write down one or more steps you will take to move you closer to what you envision.

Week of _____

	M	T	W	T	F	S	S
SPIRITUAL							
RELATIONSHIP							
HEALTH/FITNESS							
FINANCIAL							
BUSINESS/CAREER							
MINISTRY/SERVICE							
EDUCATION							
	WORD OF THE DAY:	WORD OF THE DAY:	WORD OF THE DAY:	WORD OF THE DAY:	WORD OF THE DAY:	WORD OF THE DAY:	WORD OF THE DAY:

Projects	Desired Outcomes	Deadline

To-Do List
Errands, emails, phone calls, etc.

☐ _____
☐ _____
☐ _____
☐ _____
☐ _____
☐ _____
☐ _____
☐ _____
☐ _____
☐ _____
☐ _____
☐ _____
☐ _____
☐ _____

☐ _____
☐ _____
☐ _____
☐ _____
☐ _____
☐ _____
☐ _____
☐ _____
☐ _____
☐ _____
☐ _____
☐ _____
☐ _____
☐ _____

Quick Note

Prayer Requests & Concerns

_____
_____
_____
_____
_____
_____
_____
_____
_____
_____
_____
_____
_____
_____
_____
_____
_____
_____
_____
_____
_____

Daily Bible Reading Plan

MON _____

TUE _____

WED _____

THUR _____

FRI _____

SAT _____

SUN _____

Scriptures that speak to me

My Weekly "I AM" Statements

I AM: _____

I AM: _____

I AM: _____

I AM: _____

I AM: _____

Spiritual Downloads

Record what you saw or heard in the Spirit this week regarding God's vision for your life.

Divine Expectations	Praise Report
_____	_____
_____	_____
_____	_____
_____	_____
_____	_____
_____	_____
_____	_____

My Weekly "I WILL" Statements

I WILL: _____

I WILL: _____

I WILL: _____

I WILL: _____

I WILL: _____

My Next Step Strategy
For each category, each day write down one or more steps you will take to move you closer to what you envision.

	M	T	W	T	F	S	S
SPIRITUAL							
RELATIONSHIP							
HEALTH/FITNESS							
FINANCIAL							
BUSINESS/CAREER							
MINISTRY/SERVICE							
EDUCATION							
	WORD OF THE DAY:	WORD OF THE DAY:	WORD OF THE DAY:	WORD OF THE DAY:	WORD OF THE DAY:	WORD OF THE DAY:	WORD OF THE DAY:

Week of _____

Projects	Desired Outcomes	Deadline

To-Do List
Errands, emails, phone calls, etc.

☐ _____
☐ _____
☐ _____
☐ _____
☐ _____
☐ _____
☐ _____
☐ _____
☐ _____
☐ _____
☐ _____
☐ _____
☐ _____
☐ _____
☐ _____

☐ _____
☐ _____
☐ _____
☐ _____
☐ _____
☐ _____
☐ _____
☐ _____
☐ _____
☐ _____
☐ _____
☐ _____
☐ _____
☐ _____
☐ _____

Quick Note

Prayer Requests & Concerns

_____
_____
_____
_____
_____
_____
_____
_____
_____
_____
_____
_____
_____
_____
_____
_____
_____
_____
_____
_____

Daily Bible Reading Plan

MON _____

TUE _____

WED _____

THUR _____

FRI _____

SAT _____

SUN _____

Scriptures that speak to me

My Weekly "I AM" Statements

I AM: _____

I AM: _____

I AM: _____

I AM: _____

I AM: _____

Spiritual Downloads

Record what you saw or heard in the Spirit this week regarding God's vision for your life.

Divine Expectations	Praise Report
_____	_____
_____	_____
_____	_____
_____	_____
_____	_____
_____	_____
_____	_____

My Weekly "I WILL" Statements

I WILL: _____

I WILL: _____

I WILL: _____

I WILL: _____

I WILL: _____

My Next Step Strategy

For each category, each day write down one or more steps you will take to move you closer to what you envision.

Week of _____

	M	T	W	T	F	S	S
SPIRITUAL							
RELATIONSHIP							
HEALTH/FITNESS							
FINANCIAL							
BUSINESS/CAREER							
MINISTRY/SERVICE							
EDUCATION							
	WORD OF THE DAY:	WORD OF THE DAY:	WORD OF THE DAY:	WORD OF THE DAY:	WORD OF THE DAY:	WORD OF THE DAY:	WORD OF THE DAY:

Projects	Desired Outcomes	Deadline

To-Do List
Errands, emails, phone calls, etc.

☐ _____
☐ _____
☐ _____
☐ _____
☐ _____
☐ _____
☐ _____
☐ _____
☐ _____
☐ _____
☐ _____
☐ _____
☐ _____
☐ _____

☐ _____
☐ _____
☐ _____
☐ _____
☐ _____
☐ _____
☐ _____
☐ _____
☐ _____
☐ _____
☐ _____
☐ _____
☐ _____
☐ _____

Quick Note

Prayer Requests & Concerns

_____
_____
_____
_____
_____
_____
_____
_____
_____
_____
_____
_____
_____
_____
_____
_____
_____
_____
_____
_____

Daily Bible Reading Plan

MON _____

TUE _____

WED _____

THUR _____

FRI _____

SAT _____

SUN _____

Scriptures that speak to me

My Weekly "I AM" Statements

I AM: _____

I AM: _____

I AM: _____

I AM: _____

I AM: _____

Spiritual Downloads

Record what you saw or heard in the Spirit this week regarding God's vision for your life.

Divine Expectations	Praise Report
_____	_____
_____	_____
_____	_____
_____	_____
_____	_____
_____	_____
_____	_____

My Weekly "I WILL" Statements

I WILL: _____

I WILL: _____

I WILL: _____

I WILL: _____

I WILL: _____

My Next Step Strategy

For each category, each day write down one or more steps you will take to move you closer to what you envision.

Week of _____

	M	T	W	T	F	S	S
SPIRITUAL							
RELATIONSHIP							
HEALTH/FITNESS							
FINANCIAL							
BUSINESS/CAREER							
MINISTRY/SERVICE							
EDUCATION							
	WORD OF THE DAY:	WORD OF THE DAY:	WORD OF THE DAY:	WORD OF THE DAY:	WORD OF THE DAY:	WORD OF THE DAY:	WORD OF THE DAY:

Projects	Desired Outcomes	Deadline

To-Do List
Errands, emails, phone calls, etc.

- ☐ _____
- ☐ _____
- ☐ _____
- ☐ _____
- ☐ _____
- ☐ _____
- ☐ _____
- ☐ _____
- ☐ _____
- ☐ _____
- ☐ _____
- ☐ _____
- ☐ _____
- ☐ _____
- ☐ _____

- ☐ _____
- ☐ _____
- ☐ _____
- ☐ _____
- ☐ _____
- ☐ _____
- ☐ _____
- ☐ _____
- ☐ _____
- ☐ _____
- ☐ _____
- ☐ _____
- ☐ _____
- ☐ _____
- ☐ _____

Quick Note

Prayer Requests & Concerns

_____
_____
_____
_____
_____
_____
_____
_____
_____
_____
_____
_____
_____
_____
_____
_____
_____
_____
_____
_____
_____
_____

Daily Bible Reading Plan

MON _____

TUE _____

WED _____

THUR _____

FRI _____

SAT _____

SUN _____

Scriptures that speak to me

My Weekly "I AM" Statements

I AM: _____

I AM: _____

I AM: _____

I AM: _____

I AM: _____

Spiritual Downloads

Record what you saw or heard in the Spirit this week regarding God's vision for your life.

Divine Expectations	Praise Report
_____	_____
_____	_____
_____	_____
_____	_____
_____	_____
_____	_____
_____	_____

My Weekly "I WILL" Statements

I WILL: _____

I WILL: _____

I WILL: _____

I WILL: _____

I WILL: _____

My Next Step Strategy

For each category, each day write down one or more steps you will take to move you closer to what you envision.

Week of _____

	M	T	W	T	F	S	S
SPIRITUAL							
RELATIONSHIP							
HEALTH/FITNESS							
FINANCIAL							
BUSINESS/CAREER							
MINISTRY/SERVICE							
EDUCATION							
	WORD OF THE DAY:	WORD OF THE DAY:	WORD OF THE DAY:	WORD OF THE DAY:	WORD OF THE DAY:	WORD OF THE DAY:	WORD OF THE DAY:

Projects	Desired Outcomes	Deadline

To-Do List
Errands, emails, phone calls, etc.

☐ _____
☐ _____
☐ _____
☐ _____
☐ _____
☐ _____
☐ _____
☐ _____
☐ _____
☐ _____
☐ _____
☐ _____
☐ _____
☐ _____

☐ _____
☐ _____
☐ _____
☐ _____
☐ _____
☐ _____
☐ _____
☐ _____
☐ _____
☐ _____
☐ _____
☐ _____
☐ _____
☐ _____

Quick Note

Prayer Requests & Concerns

_____
_____
_____
_____
_____
_____
_____
_____
_____
_____
_____
_____
_____
_____
_____
_____
_____
_____
_____
_____

Daily Bible Reading Plan

MON _____

TUE _____

WED _____

THUR _____

FRI _____

SAT _____

SUN _____

Scriptures that speak to me

My Weekly "I AM" Statements

I AM: _____

I AM: _____

I AM: _____

I AM: _____

I AM: _____

Spiritual Downloads

Record what you saw or heard in the Spirit this week regarding God's vision for your life.

Divine Expectations	Praise Report
_____	_____
_____	_____
_____	_____
_____	_____
_____	_____
_____	_____
_____	_____

My Weekly "I WILL" Statements

I WILL: _____

I WILL: _____

I WILL: _____

I WILL: _____

I WILL: _____

My Next Step Strategy

For each category, each day write down one or more steps you will take to move you closer to what you envision.

Week of _____

	M	T	W	T	F	S	S
SPIRITUAL							
RELATIONSHIP							
HEALTH/FITNESS							
FINANCIAL							
BUSINESS/CAREER							
MINISTRY/SERVICE							
EDUCATION							
	WORD OF THE DAY:	WORD OF THE DAY:	WORD OF THE DAY:	WORD OF THE DAY:	WORD OF THE DAY:	WORD OF THE DAY:	WORD OF THE DAY:

Projects	Desired Outcomes	Deadline

To-Do List
Errands, emails, phone calls, etc.

☐_____
☐_____
☐_____
☐_____
☐_____
☐_____
☐_____
☐_____
☐_____
☐_____
☐_____
☐_____
☐_____
☐_____

☐_____
☐_____
☐_____
☐_____
☐_____
☐_____
☐_____
☐_____
☐_____
☐_____
☐_____
☐_____
☐_____
☐_____

Quick Note

Prayer Requests & Concerns

_____
_____
_____
_____
_____
_____
_____
_____
_____
_____
_____
_____
_____
_____
_____
_____
_____
_____
_____
_____
_____

Daily Bible Reading Plan

MON _____

TUE _____

WED _____

THUR _____

FRI _____

SAT _____

SUN _____

Scriptures that speak to me

My Weekly "I AM" Statements

I AM: _____

I AM: _____

I AM: _____

I AM: _____

I AM: _____

Spiritual Downloads

Record what you saw or heard in the Spirit this week regarding God's vision for your life.

Divine Expectations	Praise Report
_____	_____
_____	_____
_____	_____
_____	_____
_____	_____
_____	_____
_____	

My Weekly "I WILL" Statements

I WILL: _____

I WILL: _____

I WILL: _____

I WILL: _____

I WILL: _____

My Next Step Strategy

For each category, each day write down one or more steps you will take to move you closer to what you envision.

Week of _____

	M	T	W	T	F	S	S
SPIRITUAL							
RELATIONSHIP							
HEALTH/FITNESS							
FINANCIAL							
BUSINESS/CAREER							
MINISTRY/SERVICE							
EDUCATION							
	WORD OF THE DAY:	WORD OF THE DAY:	WORD OF THE DAY:	WORD OF THE DAY:	WORD OF THE DAY:	WORD OF THE DAY:	WORD OF THE DAY:

Projects	Desired Outcomes	Deadline

To-Do List
Errands, emails, phone calls, etc.

☐ _____
☐ _____
☐ _____
☐ _____
☐ _____
☐ _____
☐ _____
☐ _____
☐ _____
☐ _____
☐ _____
☐ _____
☐ _____
☐ _____
☐ _____

☐ _____
☐ _____
☐ _____
☐ _____
☐ _____
☐ _____
☐ _____
☐ _____
☐ _____
☐ _____
☐ _____
☐ _____
☐ _____
☐ _____
☐ _____

Quick Note

Prayer Requests & Concerns

_____
_____
_____
_____
_____
_____
_____
_____
_____
_____
_____
_____
_____
_____
_____
_____
_____
_____
_____
_____
_____

Daily Bible Reading Plan

MON _____

TUE _____

WED _____

THUR _____

FRI _____

SAT _____

SUN _____

Scriptures that speak to me

My Weekly "I AM" Statements

I AM: _____

I AM: _____

I AM: _____

I AM: _____

I AM: _____

Spiritual Downloads

Record what you saw or heard in the Spirit this week regarding God's vision for your life.

Divine Expectations	Praise Report
_____	_____
_____	_____
_____	_____
_____	_____
_____	_____
_____	_____

My Weekly "I WILL" Statements

I WILL: _____

I WILL: _____

I WILL: _____

I WILL: _____

I WILL: _____

My Next Step Strategy
For each category, each day write down one or more steps you will take to move you closer to what you envision.

	M	T	W	T	F	S	S
SPIRITUAL							
RELATIONSHIP							
HEALTH/FITNESS							
FINANCIAL							
BUSINESS/CAREER							
MINISTRY/SERVICE							
EDUCATION							
	WORD OF THE DAY:	WORD OF THE DAY:	WORD OF THE DAY:	WORD OF THE DAY:	WORD OF THE DAY:	WORD OF THE DAY:	WORD OF THE DAY:

Week of _____

Projects	Desired Outcomes	Deadline

To-Do List
Errands, emails, phone calls, etc.

☐ _____
☐ _____
☐ _____
☐ _____
☐ _____
☐ _____
☐ _____
☐ _____
☐ _____
☐ _____
☐ _____
☐ _____
☐ _____

☐ _____
☐ _____
☐ _____
☐ _____
☐ _____
☐ _____
☐ _____
☐ _____
☐ _____
☐ _____
☐ _____
☐ _____
☐ _____

Quick Note

Prayer Requests & Concerns

_____
_____
_____
_____
_____
_____
_____
_____
_____
_____
_____
_____
_____
_____
_____
_____
_____
_____
_____
_____

Daily Bible Reading Plan

MON _____

TUE _____

WED _____

THUR _____

FRI _____

SAT _____

SUN _____

Scriptures that speak to me

My Weekly "I AM" Statements

I AM: _____

I AM: _____

I AM: _____

I AM: _____

I AM: _____

Spiritual Downloads

Record what you saw or heard in the Spirit this week regarding God's vision for your life.

Divine Expectations	Praise Report
_____	_____

My Weekly "I WILL" Statements

I WILL: _____

I WILL: _____

I WILL: _____

I WILL: _____

I WILL: _____

My Next Step Strategy

For each category, each day write down one or more steps you will take to move you closer to what you envision.

Week of _____

	M	T	W	T	F	S	S
SPIRITUAL							
RELATIONSHIP							
HEALTH/FITNESS							
FINANCIAL							
BUSINESS/CAREER							
MINISTRY/SERVICE							
EDUCATION							
	WORD OF THE DAY:	WORD OF THE DAY:	WORD OF THE DAY:	WORD OF THE DAY:	WORD OF THE DAY:	WORD OF THE DAY:	WORD OF THE DAY:

Projects	Desired Outcomes	Deadline

To-Do List
Errands, emails, phone calls, etc.

- ☐ _____
- ☐ _____
- ☐ _____
- ☐ _____
- ☐ _____
- ☐ _____
- ☐ _____
- ☐ _____
- ☐ _____
- ☐ _____
- ☐ _____
- ☐ _____
- ☐ _____
- ☐ _____
- ☐ _____

- ☐ _____
- ☐ _____
- ☐ _____
- ☐ _____
- ☐ _____
- ☐ _____
- ☐ _____
- ☐ _____
- ☐ _____
- ☐ _____
- ☐ _____
- ☐ _____
- ☐ _____
- ☐ _____
- ☐ _____

Quick Note

Prayer Requests & Concerns

_____
_____
_____
_____
_____
_____
_____
_____
_____
_____
_____
_____
_____
_____
_____
_____
_____
_____
_____
_____

Daily Bible Reading Plan

MON _____

TUE _____

WED _____

THUR _____

FRI _____

SAT _____

SUN _____

Scriptures that speak to me

My Weekly "I AM" Statements

I AM: _____

I AM: _____

I AM: _____

I AM: _____

I AM: _____

Spiritual Downloads

Record what you saw or heard in the Spirit this week regarding God's vision for your life.

Divine Expectations	Praise Report
_____	_____
_____	_____
_____	_____
_____	_____
_____	_____
_____	_____
_____	_____

My Weekly "I WILL" Statements

I WILL: _____

I WILL: _____

I WILL: _____

I WILL: _____

I WILL: _____

My Next Step Strategy

For each category, each day write down one or more steps you will take to move you closer to what you envision.

Week of _____

	M	T	W	T	F	S	S
SPIRITUAL							
RELATIONSHIP							
HEALTH/FITNESS							
FINANCIAL							
BUSINESS/CAREER							
MINISTRY/SERVICE							
EDUCATION							
	WORD OF THE DAY:	WORD OF THE DAY:	WORD OF THE DAY:	WORD OF THE DAY:	WORD OF THE DAY:	WORD OF THE DAY:	WORD OF THE DAY:

Projects	Desired Outcomes	Deadline

To-Do List
Errands, emails, phone calls, etc.

☐ _____
☐ _____
☐ _____
☐ _____
☐ _____
☐ _____
☐ _____
☐ _____
☐ _____
☐ _____
☐ _____
☐ _____
☐ _____
☐ _____

☐ _____
☐ _____
☐ _____
☐ _____
☐ _____
☐ _____
☐ _____
☐ _____
☐ _____
☐ _____
☐ _____
☐ _____
☐ _____
☐ _____

Quick Note

Prayer Requests & Concerns

_____

_____

_____

_____

_____

_____

_____

_____

_____

_____

_____

_____

_____

_____

_____

_____

_____

_____

_____

_____

_____

Daily Bible Reading Plan

MON _____

TUE _____

WED _____

THUR _____

FRI _____

SAT _____

SUN _____

Scriptures that speak to me

My Weekly "I AM" Statements

I AM: _____

I AM: _____

I AM: _____

I AM: _____

I AM: _____

Spiritual Downloads

Record what you saw or heard in the Spirit this week regarding God's vision for your life.

Divine Expectations

_____
_____
_____
_____
_____
_____
_____

Praise Report

_____
_____
_____
_____
_____
_____
_____

My Weekly "I WILL" Statements

I WILL: _____

I WILL: _____

I WILL: _____

I WILL: _____

I WILL: _____

My Next Step Strategy

For each category, each day write down one or more steps you will take to move you closer to what you envision.

Week of _____

	M	T	W	T	F	S	S
SPIRITUAL							
RELATIONSHIP							
HEALTH/FITNESS							
FINANCIAL							
BUSINESS/CAREER							
MINISTRY/SERVICE							
EDUCATION							
	WORD OF THE DAY:	WORD OF THE DAY:	WORD OF THE DAY:	WORD OF THE DAY:	WORD OF THE DAY:	WORD OF THE DAY:	WORD OF THE DAY:

Projects	Desired Outcomes	Deadline

To-Do List
Errands, emails, phone calls, etc.

- ☐ _____
- ☐ _____
- ☐ _____
- ☐ _____
- ☐ _____
- ☐ _____
- ☐ _____
- ☐ _____
- ☐ _____
- ☐ _____
- ☐ _____
- ☐ _____
- ☐ _____
- ☐ _____
- ☐ _____

- ☐ _____
- ☐ _____
- ☐ _____
- ☐ _____
- ☐ _____
- ☐ _____
- ☐ _____
- ☐ _____
- ☐ _____
- ☐ _____
- ☐ _____
- ☐ _____
- ☐ _____
- ☐ _____
- ☐ _____

Quick Note

Prayer Requests & Concerns

_____
_____
_____
_____
_____
_____
_____
_____
_____
_____
_____
_____
_____
_____
_____
_____
_____
_____
_____
_____
_____

Daily Bible Reading Plan

MON _____

TUE _____

WED _____

THUR _____

FRI _____

SAT _____

SUN _____

Scriptures that speak to me

My Weekly "I AM" Statements

I AM: _____

I AM: _____

I AM: _____

I AM: _____

I AM: _____

Spiritual Downloads

Record what you saw or heard in the Spirit this week regarding God's vision for your life.

Divine Expectations	Praise Report
_____	_____
_____	_____
_____	_____
_____	_____
_____	_____
_____	_____
_____	_____

My Weekly "I WILL" Statements

I WILL: _____

I WILL: _____

I WILL: _____

I WILL: _____

I WILL: _____

My Next Step Strategy

For each category, each day write down one or more steps you will take to move you closer to what you envision.

	M	T	W	T	F	S	S
SPIRITUAL							
RELATIONSHIP							
HEALTH/FITNESS							
FINANCIAL							
BUSINESS/CAREER							
MINISTRY/SERVICE							
EDUCATION							
	WORD OF THE DAY:	WORD OF THE DAY:	WORD OF THE DAY:	WORD OF THE DAY:	WORD OF THE DAY:	WORD OF THE DAY:	WORD OF THE DAY:

Week of _____

Projects	Desired Outcomes	Deadline

To-Do List
Errands, emails, phone calls, etc.

- ☐ _____
- ☐ _____
- ☐ _____
- ☐ _____
- ☐ _____
- ☐ _____
- ☐ _____
- ☐ _____
- ☐ _____
- ☐ _____
- ☐ _____
- ☐ _____
- ☐ _____
- ☐ _____

- ☐ _____
- ☐ _____
- ☐ _____
- ☐ _____
- ☐ _____
- ☐ _____
- ☐ _____
- ☐ _____
- ☐ _____
- ☐ _____
- ☐ _____
- ☐ _____
- ☐ _____
- ☐ _____

Quick Note

Prayer Requests & Concerns

_____
_____
_____
_____
_____
_____
_____
_____
_____
_____
_____
_____
_____
_____
_____
_____
_____
_____
_____
_____
_____

Daily Bible Reading Plan

MON _____

TUE _____

WED _____

THUR _____

FRI _____

SAT _____

SUN _____

Scriptures that speak to me

My Weekly "I AM" Statements

I AM: _____

I AM: _____

I AM: _____

I AM: _____

I AM: _____

Spiritual Downloads

Record what you saw or heard in the Spirit this week regarding God's vision for your life.

Divine Expectations	Praise Report
_____	_____
_____	_____
_____	_____
_____	_____
_____	_____
_____	_____
_____	_____

My Weekly "I WILL" Statements

I WILL: _____

I WILL: _____

I WILL: _____

I WILL: _____

I WILL: _____

My Next Step Strategy

For each category, each day write down one or more steps you will take to move you closer to what you envision.

Week of _____

	M	T	W	T	F	S	S
SPIRITUAL							
RELATIONSHIP							
HEALTH/FITNESS							
FINANCIAL							
BUSINESS/CAREER							
MINISTRY/SERVICE							
EDUCATION	WORD OF THE DAY:	WORD OF THE DAY:	WORD OF THE DAY:	WORD OF THE DAY:	WORD OF THE DAY:	WORD OF THE DAY:	WORD OF THE DAY:

Projects	Desired Outcomes	Deadline

To-Do List
Errands, emails, phone calls, etc.

- ☐ _____
- ☐ _____
- ☐ _____
- ☐ _____
- ☐ _____
- ☐ _____
- ☐ _____
- ☐ _____
- ☐ _____
- ☐ _____
- ☐ _____
- ☐ _____
- ☐ _____
- ☐ _____
- ☐ _____

- ☐ _____
- ☐ _____
- ☐ _____
- ☐ _____
- ☐ _____
- ☐ _____
- ☐ _____
- ☐ _____
- ☐ _____
- ☐ _____
- ☐ _____
- ☐ _____
- ☐ _____
- ☐ _____
- ☐ _____

Quick Note

Prayer Requests & Concerns

_____
_____
_____
_____
_____
_____
_____
_____
_____
_____
_____
_____
_____
_____
_____
_____
_____
_____
_____
_____

Daily Bible Reading Plan

MON _____

TUE _____

WED _____

THUR _____

FRI _____

SAT _____

SUN _____

Scriptures that speak to me

My Weekly "I AM" Statements

I AM: _____

I AM: _____

I AM: _____

I AM: _____

I AM: _____

Spiritual Downloads

Record what you saw or heard in the Spirit this week regarding God's vision for your life.

Divine Expectations	Praise Report
_____	_____
_____	_____
_____	_____
_____	_____
_____	_____
_____	_____
_____	_____

My Weekly "I WILL" Statements

I WILL: _____

I WILL: _____

I WILL: _____

I WILL: _____

I WILL: _____

GREAT THINGS NEVER HAPPEN BY ACCIDENT.

FIRST IT'S ENVISIONED, **SECONDLY, PLANNED,** AND THEN EXECUTED.

EXECUTE THE VISION:

MY MAJOR PROJECTS FOR THE YEAR

MY MONTHLY FINANCE TRACKER

ENTERTAINMENT & ENRICHMENT

INSPIRATION & MOTIVATION

MY GRATITUDE JOURNAL

EXECUTING THE VISION:
My major projects for the year

VISION/GOAL: _____ DATE: _____

My Objective:	Completion dates
Key Action Steps	

Who can help me?	Products & services I need:

Projected cost:

Notes

To Do - Summary

My Accountability Partner

EXECUTING THE VISION:
My major projects for the year

VISION/GOAL: _____ DATE: _____

My Objective:	Completion dates
Key Action Steps	

Who can help me?

Products & services I need:

Projected cost:

Notes

To Do - Summary

My Accountability Partner

EXECUTING THE VISION:
My major projects for the year

VISION/GOAL: _____ DATE: _____

My Objective:	Completion dates

Key Action Steps

Who can help me?

Products & services I need:

Projected cost:

Notes

Ideas • Inspiration • Questions

To Do - Summary

My Accountability Partner

EXECUTING THE VISION:
My major projects for the year

VISION/GOAL: _____ DATE: _____

My Objective:		Completion dates
Key Action Steps		

Who can help me?	Products & services I need:

Projected cost:

Notes

To Do - Summary

My Accountability Partner

EXECUTING THE VISION:
My major projects for the year

VISION/GOAL: _____ DATE: _____

My Objective:		Completion dates
Key Action Steps		

Who can help me?	Products & services I need:

Projected cost:

Notes

To Do - Summary

My Accountability Partner

EXECUTING THE VISION:
My major projects for the year

VISION/GOAL: _____ DATE: _____

My Objective:	Completion dates
Key Action Steps	

Who can help me?	Products & services I need:

Projected cost:

Notes

To Do - Summary

My Accountability Partner

MY MONTHLY FINANCE TRACKER

BILLS/PAYMENTS	JAN	FEB	MAR	APR	MAY	JUN
TOTAL						

Emergency Savings						
Retirement Savings						
Personal Savings						
Project Savings						
INCOME						
EXPENSES & SAVINGS						
MONEY LEFT						

MY MONTHLY FINANCE TRACKER

BILLS/PAYMENTS	JUL	AUG	SEPT	OCT	NOV	DEC
TOTAL						

Emergency Savings						
Retirement Savings						
Personal Savings						
Project Savings						
INCOME						
EXPENSES & SAVINGS						
MONEY LEFT						

ENRICHMENT & ENTERTAINMENT

Books to read	Movies & documentaries to watch

Places to visit

ENRICHMENT & ENTERTAINMENT

What I would do if I had no limitations?

Courses to take

INSPIRATION & MOTIVATION

People that inspire me
_____
_____
_____
_____
_____
_____
_____
_____
_____
_____
_____
_____
_____
_____
_____

Things that inspire me
_____
_____
_____
_____
_____
_____
_____
_____
_____
_____
_____
_____
_____
_____
_____

Websites to remember
_____
_____
_____
_____
_____

INSPIRATION & MOTIVATION

My Bucket List

_____   _____
_____   _____
_____   _____
_____   _____
_____   _____
_____   _____
_____   _____
_____   _____
_____   _____
_____   _____
_____   _____
_____   _____
_____   _____
_____   _____
_____   _____

Conferences & retreats to attend

_____
_____
_____
_____

In everything give thanks; for this is the will of God in Christ Jesus for you.
I Thessalonians 5:18

In everything give thanks; for this is the will of God in Christ Jesus for you.
I Thessalonians 5:18

In everything give thanks; for this is the will of God in Christ Jesus for you.
I Thessalonians 5:18

In everything give thanks; for this is the will of God in Christ Jesus for you.
I Thessalonians 5:18

In everything give thanks; for this is the will of God in Christ Jesus for you.
I Thessalonians 5:18

In everything give thanks; for this is the will of God in Christ Jesus for you.
I Thessalonians 5:18

In everything give thanks; for this is the will of God in Christ Jesus for you.
I Thessalonians 5:18

In everything give thanks; for this is the will of God in Christ Jesus for you.
I Thessalonians 5:18

FOR THE VISION IS YET
FOR AN APPOINTED TIME
BUT AT THE END
IT WILL SPEAK,
AND IT WILL NOT LIE.

THOUGH IT TARRIES,
WAIT FOR IT; BECAUSE
IT WILL SURELY COME

IT WILL NOT TARRY.

HABUKKUK 2:3

Order more copies of this journal-planner at:
www.MyNextStepVisionBoardJournal.com
and where books are sold.